Expect *the* *Miraculous*

A True Life Story of the
Extraordinary Power of God

---

by
Carol Romeo

Copyright © 2022 by Carol Romeo.

ISBN 978-1-64133-726-7 (softcover)
ISBN 978-1-64133-727-4 (ebook)

All rights reserved. No part of this book may be reproduced or transmitted in any form or by any means, electronic or mechanical, including photocopying, recording, or by any information storage and retrieval system without express written permission from the author, except in the case of brief quotations embodied in critical reviews and certain other noncommercial uses permitted by copyright law.

Printed in the United States of America.

Brilliant Books Literary
137 Forest Park Lane Thomasville
North Carolina 27360 USA

*This book is dedicated to my Mama,
Irene H. Pearsall
Whose love for me remained constant
and brought healing beyond words.*

Contents

Introduction vii

Section I: Life-Changing Miracles
    Chapter One: Jesus the Savior 4
    Chapter Two: Jesus the Healer 11
    Chapter Three: The Holy Spirit 18
    Chapter Four: Jesus' Appearance 25
    Chapter Five: Jesus Heals our Addictions 34
    Chapter Six: Angelic Protection 41
    Chapter Seven: Deliverance 50
    Chapter Eight: Healing of the Heart 57

Section II: Increasing Our Hunger
    Chapter Nine: Prayer 68
    Chapter Ten: Mystical Vision 73
    Chapter Eleven: Surprised by Joy 80
    Chapter Twelve: Depression Healed 87
    Chapter Thirteen: Mountainside Experience 93
    Chapter Fourteen: Raised from the Dead 97
    Chapter Fifteen: Gold Teeth 102
    Chapter Sixteen: The Comforter 109

Section III: Divine Purpose: PREPARE
    Chapter Seventeen: Prayers of Intercession 118
    Chapter Eighteen: Repentance 125

Chapter Nineteen: Expectation 130
Chapter Twenty: Press In 137
Chapter Twenty-One: Be Aware 145
Chapter Twenty-Two: Resurrect 153
Chapter Twenty-Three: Exercise 160

Epilogue 168
Scripture References 175
References 176

Introduction

Our God is a wondrous, supernatural God who desires to impart His miracle working power to each one of you. Throughout this book, I will describe my personal experiences with miracles, as well as the ones that He imparted through me for others. Both experiences shaped my relationship with the Lord in a vibrant, exciting journey which propelled me deeper and deeper into the magnificent heartbeat of God towards me.

Throughout the many decades of getting to know the Lord Jesus, I have discovered that He is truly supernatural. He is always desirous of reaching into our natural world and impacting us with His supernatural nature. It is His desire that we know Him intimately—His ways and His love.

He has chosen to reveal Himself to me in many varied ways. The most exciting to me have been the miraculous—those times when I actually had the privilege of experiencing the wonder of His Spirit healing or transforming me. He also offers smaller miracles that are just as supernatural, but we may miss them if we are not looking for them.

In Jesus' quest for opportunities to uncover Himself to us and reveal the hidden nature of His Spirit, I believe that His main goal is *relationship*. He wants us to *know* Him intimately and be *known* by Him. Belonging is what our spiritual walk is all about. As Jesus reveals more of His nature to us, and we reciprocate by opening to His Spirit, we become joined in the spiritual realm.

Jesus Christ came to be born on this earth to show us that we are not alone—that there is a spiritual world we can be part of—and that we are meant to be part of. When He left this earth He gave us His Holy Spirit so that we could remain attached to Him and continue to learn of Him.

One more thing that simply stretches my thinking, "As we stay attached to Him, His Spirit gives us the power to perform the same supernatural feats that He performed while on this earth." That alone is amazing. But for me, the most amazing experience is the privilege of relationship with the Almighty God, and inside that relationship, the power to be transformed into His image.

Through these pages you will see the many facets of our Lord Jesus and the many ways He has of revealing Himself to us and through us. I hope you will see, through my responses to the Lord in the various occurrences, that our response to His Spirit is a vital part of the transformation that Christ wants to bring to us.

In Sections I and II, you will get an inside look at the miracles which I and my family experienced. With every touch on my life, He redeemed me, delivered me, healed me, transformed me, created in me a hunger for Him that would never die. He loved me until I couldn't help but love Him back. That is the supernatural.

In these sections I will also provide you with a look at my character growth because of Him. You will see how my hungry heart kept me open for everything the Lord desired to bless me with and the way His love engaged my heart propelling me to want more. *I believe every action of God is directed towards captivating us with His love. It is love in action. The miraculous experience is pregnant with the possibility of knowing this love in a greater measure.*

In Section III, using the acronym PREPARE, I will outline some of the ways you can *prepare* for what God wants to do in and through you. You will see the ways I needed to align myself with God's calling on my life and some of the ways the Holy

Spirit used me to perform miracles in others. God's miracles are still in His hands to release, but you and I are the vessels He may use to complete them.

The Epilogue closes my book with one of the most recent, gentle miracles I have experienced and a look at how it uncovered the depth of God's graciousness extended to me. It was, indeed, a very loving period at the end of four decades of walking with and serving my Lord.

The experiences that I share are just how they occurred. It may seem like I am lifting up the supernatural above the natural, but I am aware that God meets us in many varied ways, subtle and miraculous. He is a big God who, I believe, desires for us to know Him in His bigness. If we overlook the miraculous, we are leaving out an important part of the very nature of God. When Jesus came in the flesh, He came to reveal God. One of the ways He did that was through moving in the miraculous:

> *And when Jesus went out He saw a great multitude; and He was **moved with compassion** for them, and healed their sick. (Matthew 14:14 NKJ)*

Jesus' intention is very clear. He not only revealed to humanity that He/God possessed the power to miraculously heal and transform them, but within this experience they would come to know His love. We then have the power to complete the dynamic experience by returning the love He has given us. Our encounter than accomplishes what God intends all along—to be united with Christ in His love.

My desire is that your heart will begin to hunger for God and, having done so, will continue to increase your appetite for more of the Lord. That is one of my main reasons for writing this book. I want to share with you the "more" of God that I have experienced to stir your heart and awaken your knowledge that there is more that God has for you.

Whether you have not yet begun your walk with the Lord or have walked with Him for many decades, He still has more for you. In the supernatural realm there are no limitations and God never tires of giving His graces. This is my prayer and praise. Can you let it be yours?

> *I will thank the Lord with all my heart as I meet with his godly people. How amazing are the deeds of the Lord! All who delight in him should ponder them. Everything he does reveals his glory and majesty. His righteousness never fails. (Psalm 111: 1–3 NLT)*

Section I

Life-Changing Miracles

God's intention is always to *impart new life* to us. Then how can two people experiencing the same miracle have differing outcomes? One person can be radically changed and the other may be affected minimally or not at all. The two people may experience the same thing, but process it and respond to it differently.

The process of experiencing and integrating miracles has to do with our cognitive functioning and the responses of our emotions. How we process is influenced by a myriad of factors: education, church exposure, culture, parental ideology, previous experiences, personality, emotional stability or instability. As I share my supernatural experiences with you, I will share both my cognitive and emotional responses. I invite you to reflect on the ways that you might process these spiritual experiences. How might this process affect your relationship with the Lord?

A vital question to ask yourself is, "What is Christ's overarching goal?" In other words, "What is God's intention for granting this miracle at this time? What does He want me to recognize about Him, learn or change about myself?" I believe His goal, in general, has a two part function. First, He wants us to know Him and His love for us, so we will return the love and, therefore, enter a relationship with Him. Second, He wants us to know Him and His love for us, so we will be changed into His image and be able to share His love with others on this earth.

> *Long ago, even before he made the world, God loved us and chose us in Christ to be holy and without fault in his eyes. His unchanging plan has always been to adopt us into his own family by bringing us to himself through Jesus Christ. And this gave him great pleasure. (Ephesians 1:4–5 NLT)*

God's intention is always to share His love, but when we encounter that love, we get to choose how to react—how to react in our relationship with Jesus and if we will allow His love to change us in ways that make us more like Him. That is why a miracle always includes you. Your response is very important.

Living the supernatural life is all about love and responding to love. Yes, there were amazing times when Jesus touched me while I was in a wayward state; however, I was always responsible to respond to His calling.

As you read my story, I hope that you can see that it was not only the miracles themselves that impacted me, but more so, it was the love of God that saturated my dry heart. Every message He brings, every healing miracle, every deliverance, every vision is soaked and saturated in His love.

Every time I experienced a wow moment with the Lord, I wondered, "Could His love get any better?" Surprisingly, very surprisingly, the answer is yes! Jesus longs for us to experience His love to a greater and greater measure because there is no end to His love. And, I have found, there is no end to the many varied ways He has to reveal His love to us.

The love of God is everything to me. As a child of the King I can't lose. You can't lose as you follow Him and turn towards Him. Even though I am not perfect in my relationship with Christ, I have learned how to turn towards Him no matter what my emotional or physical state. That was how I learned to respond, and that habit became my refuge. Your response, whatever it is, will become your story. The *unveiled love of God* is the gift inside of every miracle if you reach for it.

> *For God so loved the world that he gave his only Son, so that everyone who believes in him will not perish but have eternal life. (John 3:16 NLT)*

Chapter One

Jesus the Savior

Before I experienced the miracle of salvation, there was a part of me that didn't believe anything or anybody could fix me or the situation. I had slid so far down into this confused, agonizing, depressed state. I cried my self to sleep every night with my head buried into the pillow so my husband wouldn't hear. I didn't know what was wrong with me. I just knew that if something didn't change I couldn't go on. I had tried to commit suicide twice in my life—once when I was twelve and once as a young adult—about three years and four kids ago. I sincerely did not want to go down that road again. Thankfully, there was still a small part of me that wanted to keep searching for an answer. That led me to the Baptist Church in the town in which I lived.

As a child, I knew of Jesus. My parents took me to church even though they did not attend. I remember feeling love and peace in that place. I felt drawn to pray and I knew that Jesus was there for me. So, it was very natural that church would be the place I would begin searching for some peace. I started visiting all the churches in my neighborhood and settled at the Baptist Church.

A decade before, I had met my husband, Tony, in a nightclub in Long Island, New York. I was dancing and waiting tables, and he was a singer and manager. We quickly became involved. Both of us for different reasons were desperate for love. He was 23 years my senior and married with four children. I was young, naive and not an ounce of me rational enough to think things through. "I was in love" and that's all I needed to know.

We got pregnant and decided to move from New York to California to start a new life. I was running from my parents and he from his ex. In my fantasies I thought I was getting the dream marriage that was going to fix all the pain of my childhood.

After the first two years, I birthed our second child and we received two of Tony's four children—9 and 11 year old boys. As you can imagine, I was way over my head. Tony was caught up in earning a living and trying to resolve some of the monumental guilt he carried from initially abandoning the children. That left most of the childrearing and disciplining to me.

My over-whelm built rapidly. There I was at age 22, caring for my infant son, toddler daughter and my two step-sons. My emotions started breaking down. This was not even close to the dream marriage I had planned. I felt trapped. This nightmare was supposed to have been my salvation, while it actually felt like my demise—hence, the sleepless tearful nights.

Abuse was creeping into our family system. Tony and I were becoming verbally and at times physically abusive to one another and to the children. Our alcohol consumption was increasing. I carried the pain which came from my abusive alcoholic family of origin, but I didn't know how to stop it when it was happening again. I was desperate for a changed life.

I still wasn't sure what I needed, or if God could do anything about it, but I am so thankful that I was willing to try. Even though I did not yet know Jesus as my Savior and Redeemer, His Spirit was already at work in me drawing me to Himself and preparing my heart. I would find myself thinking about

Jesus and the fleeting amounts of connection I felt with Him as a child. Could I feel that again? Would His arms still be open to me? I didn't know I needed salvation or what salvation was, but the Spirit of God knew what I needed and He continued to draw me out to search for Him, into a loving church.

Someone asked me recently, "What is the greatest miracle you have experienced?" Without a doubt I had to say, "Salvation, of course." Salvation is the greatest supernatural happening there is because it is an instantaneous transformation of death to life—God displacing a life lived by the flesh to a life lived by the Spirit. One of the Christian terms used for this experience is being "born again." It is a great term because in the experience we actually become awakened to the spiritual beings we were always meant to be. Therefore, we are born again of the Spirit of God.

I had been attending Women's Bible Study Fellowship at the Baptist Church for over six months and was growing in the knowledge and the love of God, although I just started attending the services on Sunday mornings. This particular Sunday, I learned that there was going to be a guest preacher. Everybody in my group seemed excited about it and encouraged me to go.

When I entered the church sanctuary that morning, it seemed like there was more energy in the room than usual—unless it was my underlying anxiety. I was told the guest preacher was an evangelist. Now, I didn't know what an "evangelist" was there to do, so I felt somewhat uneasy. When he started to preach, however, I felt like I was the only one in the room. I lost all sense of what was happening around me. It was as though he was preaching right to me. God was speaking directly to me and directly into my heart. Before he even finished his message, I had tears running down my face. I knew that I needed exactly what he was talking about. I needed a new life, a changed life.

It was not only the words the preacher was speaking—I could feel, actually feel, the love of God touching my heart and offering me a new way. At that moment the preacher said, "If the

Spirit is speaking to you and you want to give your life to Jesus, come down front."

My heart was pounding. I had never felt anything like this in my life. My emotions deep within my soul were magically stirred. The excitement was building. Was it really true that God was choosing me? If He was calling me, how could I not answer His call? My body was shaking as I stood to my feet. The loving presence of the Spirit became obvious and continued to draw me as I walked to the altar and responded to the call of my Savior. I was ready to give my life over to Jesus.

I bowed my head at the altar and all the errors I had made while trying to direct my own life came flooding up. I gave God all the wrongs I had committed, and released all the pain in my heart. That day, as I stood there glued to the sanctuary floor, I made the most important choice of my life. I said, "Jesus, take my broken life and do with me what you want. I don't know how to change the things that are causing me so much pain, but maybe you do." Within that precious moment, His love met my opened heart and I felt true hope for the first time in my adult life.

As the weeks following my salvation experience unfolded, there were aspects of God's plan for me that I recognized immediately and others that came more gradually. The greatest immediate reaction was the way the Holy Spirit began drawing me into the Word of God. I had been studying the Bible for the last number of months with the Bible Study Fellowship, but this experience was different. I felt pulled or drawn into the Word with a fervency that was unmistakable.

The words that I read in the Bible came alive. They spoke to me personally and were like food for my soul. The more I read, the hungrier I became for more. I found that I couldn't read enough. His Word was lovingly penetrating the outcast places in my soul and accurately attending to my every need. And, I couldn't pray enough. My greatest delight at the end of the day was visiting with my Lord in prayer and in His Word. I could hardly wait to get there.

I was in awe at what God was doing as I felt my heart shift more every day. Just a few weeks ago, my heart and mind had been filled with confusion, pain, anger, depression and hopelessness. Now, I was filled with so much peace there was no place for those emotions. My addictive desires were changing as well. My alcohol consumption stopped completely as well as my craving for cigarettes. I realized I was going through a major transformation, although it felt so easy. That is what was so amazing to me. I knew that there was a power other than me who was doing the work.

Needless to say, my husband was beginning to take notice. Some of the changes he really enjoyed—like my newfound peace. I no longer engaged in any fighting matches with him. And my love of God, which I now felt at a deeper level, was intriguing to him. I would catch his inquisitive glances that contained a million of unspoken inquiries. The woman that he had known a short time ago was gone.

My salvation was just the beginning of my fascinating journey with my supernatural God, Jesus Christ. Every interaction with Him transformed me in greater ways. But, it is not only His ability to transform our character that is so intriguing to me—it is the privileged experience of personally getting to know this amazing God/Creator.

Our Lord God is a very big God. Every time I receive His miraculous touch, it releases in me the hunger and desire for more. And Jesus is always willing to give us more. Each encounter would draw me closer and closer to Him and into a deeper realization of His love for me. Even though we might see salvation as a one-time experience, it is actually through all of our encounters with the Lord that we come to know Him more, all of the facets of His character and especially His love.

It is an awesome experience to feel known by God. As I stood at the altar and said, "Jesus, take my life and make of it what you will," there came a deep inner feeling of relief. I felt naked before God, but at the same time I knew I was OK. I was more than OK, though. Jesus saw all of my faults and embraced me right where I was. All of the heavy burdens I carried to somehow fix myself and fix my family were lifted. I knew in that moment that I did not have to fix anything. Jesus was going to do that. To say, "I felt forgiven" is not a full enough statement. Yes, I felt forgiven, but a feeling even greater was the marvelous realization that I was "known by God." He *is* my Father and I *am* His child. There was no doubt of that in my heart—what an amazing transition!

When Jesus reaches into the natural realm with His supernatural touch, He bridges the gap between the natural and supernatural. God sees who we are and where we are. To be known—that is an important thing for us human beings to experience. When God reaches out individually to you, you are not sharing that experience with someone else. You, alone, are being impacted. When you can know that it is **God** impacting you, your relationship with God can be exquisitely transformed.

Jesus invites us into a captivating dynamic relationship with Him. That is the hunger that replaced my desperate hunger for my life to change. It is a heart hunger that is motivated and matures through His love for me and my love for Him.

This experience was the open door through which the Lord would release miracle upon miracle of His transforming grace in my life. Jesus knocked on the door of my heart that day in the Baptist Church. However, it was up to me to open the door.

My prayer is that you will *experience* throughout these pages that undying, magnificent, love of God for yourself. I believe there is an open heaven not just for me, but for you. And, if you but just crack the door open, He will come in with His abounding, relentless love. This is what Jesus has to say to you:

> *Behold, I stand at the door and knock. If anyone hears My voice and opens the door, I will come in to him and dine with him, and he with Me. (Revelation 3:20 NKJ)*

Chapter Two

Jesus the Healer

Opening the door to my Savior Jesus Christ was just the beginning of a life-transforming love relationship. There were times I would be amazed, mesmerized, shaken, grateful, humbled, curious, transfixed, awakened, cleansed. Jesus has the ability to stir these emotions and more in the hearts of His people because He is the Creator. He is always creating and always able to give something *more*.

It is each experience that draws us into the next. It is natural to want more. The psalmist tells us:

> Oh, **taste** and see that the Lord is good.
> (Psalm 34:8 NKJ)

To taste something, we must *experience* it. What happens on a physical level when we taste something that is very good? We want more! If that occurs on a physical level, how much more are our appetites stimulated when we taste of the goodness of the Lord on a supernatural level. This is the hunger that draws us forward to the more that God has for us.

After my salvation experience, I heard of a church in Anaheim called Melodyland where people were receiving healing and experiencing an occurrence called being "slain in the Spirit." (I prefer the alternative term "resting in the Spirit.") The stories I heard were of people falling to the ground while getting prayed for and that many times a miraculous healing took place. I was *very* curious. Jesus had done so many miracles in my heart already. I was in a state of heightened anticipation and ready to see what more He had for me.

I told my neighbor, Joni, a little bit about the church and we set a date for the following week. I couldn't wait. Every time I prayed about it, I experienced an excitement that bubbled up in my heart and spirit. I didn't know what God would do, but I was sure it was something amazing.

The day came and we pulled into the church parking lot, still chatting from our hour-long drive to Anaheim. I felt nervous from the exuberant anticipation of what might happen, and conversely anxious about the possibility that nothing would happen! I hadn't shared my expectations with Joni. I wasn't sure she would understand. Then, again, maybe I was afraid to put my hopes out there.

When we entered the building, Joni was not comfortable with sitting in front, so we found a couple of seats near the back of the auditorium. The congregation was just starting to worship and I could feel the presence of the Spirit, which was familiar to me, so I relaxed internally, forgetting about my nerves. Pastor Wilkerson then began to name certain illnesses and invite those people to come forward for healing. A number of people who went forward for prayer fell to the ground, "slain in the Spirit" and that peaked my interest. Some of the people claimed to be healed and there was a lot of praising and clapping at their announcement.

As the service went on, I began to feel a bit discouraged. I felt like the Spirit had directed me to come, but the preaching was coming to an end and I felt passed over. Just then, the pastor called for anyone with back problems to come forward. I wasn't even thinking about my back. I had quite severe back problems. I was seeing a chiropractor and at times wore a brace, but I just sat there.

Joni finally said, "Why don't you go up and get prayer for your back?"

I walked forward in a fog. I didn't know what to expect. When I got to the front, I told Pastor Wilkerson the problem. He asked if I also had one leg shorter than the other.

I said, "Yes, my right leg is about ¾ inch shorter."

Then he invited anyone who wanted to *see a miracle* to come down front. That comment made me more than a bit self-conscious.

I thought, "What kind of miracle are they going to see?"

Pastor Wilkerson then asked if I would sit down and let him measure my legs. I did what he asked and while he held my feet, several assistants put hands on my head and back. The pastor then spoke a prayer for healing that seemed very ordinary. Nonetheless, what I experienced in the next few moments was anything but ordinary.

It felt like a bucket of warm water was poured over my head. The warmth traveled into my neck and back as I noticed a very weird sensation. The bones in my lower back started moving and shifting position and I watched my right leg grow out to meet the left. Everyone started praising God! All I can say is that I was immediately stunned. This was not what I had expected. I never even heard of this kind of miracle before. Was this really a miracle?

When the meeting ended, a number of people came over to me and said how pleased they were that Jesus had healed me in that way. I was still in a fog. I had no prior experience with God, nor witnessed any happening like it. I *knew* God had done something because I felt it in my body, but I had no words for it as yet.

The ride home with Joni was oddly quiet. I think Joni asked some questions about my experience, but I am sure my responses were limited. I didn't know how she was categorizing what happened. I did know I needed time to sort out my feelings.

Even though I initially failed to share my story with anyone, I tested my healing over and over. Each time I sat down, I slid my fanny to the back of the chair, extended both legs out in front of me and critically examined their length. I must have persisted in measuring them dozens of times for several days. I still remained silent, but inside my head there was lots of chatter.

"What just happened to me?"

"Was this God?" I was never taught that Jesus did these kinds of miracles today.

"If this was God, why did He choose me?"

I knew what I experienced in my body, but it didn't make sense in my head. I decided to visit my chiropractor.

When I walked into the doctor's office, I had no foreknowledge of what I would tell him. I was more interested in what he would tell me. Therefore, I said, "I want you to examine me and let me know what you think."

During the exam, he was the one who was silent. He didn't do any manipulation, but he examined my back, hips and legs thoroughly. Finally, he said, "I have to know what happened to you. Get dressed and we will talk in my office." I did as he requested and when I entered his office, his full attention was on me.

I asked, "What did you find?"

It took him several minutes to answer me. He glanced down at his desk and shuffled some papers back and forth before he looked up and said,

"I don't know how to explain it." He hesitated once again.

"Your hips and leg lengths are even. Can you tell me what happened?"

So, there I was, sitting in my doctor's office, sharing my healing experience for the very first time. Somewhere within my stumbling words I used the word *miracle* and he said, "Well, I don't know too much about miracles, either, but I think this qualifies as one."

I left there feeling a little more settled about the healing that happened in my body. But I still had so many unanswered questions about God. I didn't know how to respond. I realized that God had performed a miracle in me, but I was far from recognizing the full impact of that miracle on my life and most of all, my relationship with Jesus Christ.

Sometimes when miracles happen it *takes us awhile to digest it* because the supernatural experience is so far from the reality we live in day to day. Also, if we have had religious teachings that do not include supernatural miracles, then we may have difficulty when God acts outside of the boxes we have put Him in.

Eventually, I shared my experience with my husband, Tony. He didn't outwardly respond to the news (I didn't think he would); nevertheless, he couldn't ignore the fact that I wasn't complaining of my back pain anymore and I was no longer visiting the chiropractor. Tony's curiosity over this event, and the many changes that were happening to me, moved him to silence, too.

He told me later that he was stunned and having difficulty processing. The God that he had known as a child was not a God of miracles. He grew up with the assumption that miracles only happened in biblical times. In addition, Tony was also dealing with his own heart issues with God. He was in the resisting phase, which was becoming harder and harder to maintain because of what he saw happening to me.

Eventually, this miracle and others like it, would uncover Tony's and my eyes by lifting the veil that exists between the natural and the supernatural. We would get a glimpse of who our Savior really is and His ability to show Himself through the miraculous. We accepted that Jesus is supernatural and thus He delights to reveal Himself to us through the supernatural. Look at John's disciples and the question they asked of Jesus:

> *When the men came to Jesus, they said, "John the Baptist sent us to you to ask, Are you the one who was to come, or should we expect someone else?"*
>
> *So He replied to the messengers, "Go back and report to John what you have seen and heard: The blind receive sight, the lame walk, those who have leprosy are cured, the deaf hear, the dead are raised, and the good news is preached to the poor." (Luke 7:20&22 NIV)*

What Jesus was communicating was that those miracles were a testimony of *who* He was! There was nothing else that needed to be said and there was no other proof that was necessary. Nevertheless, it can take us awhile to integrate that truth into our reality. What aided my process was spending time in God's Word and learning more about the actions of Christ while on this earth. My knowledge had to catch up with my experience.

We are mind and heart beings and as such we need to allow ourselves the time we need to process new experiences cognitively and emotionally.

When we experience the supernatural the impact is largely emotional, but we also need to support our cognitive process. The Bible needs to be an important part of creating for us the full picture of Christ. When I talk about processing a supernatural event, what I am referring to is your ability to gain a picture from the event that will expand how you see Christ, yourself in reference to Christ, and maybe even yourself in the world, discovering what God wants to teach you through the event. If we just go from one supernatural event to the next without processing, then we may be experiencing the high or the mountain top experience, but not gaining the whole picture.

Prior to my healing, I knew Christ as my Savior. Now I was learning that He also is my Healer. He purchased that rite through the stripes He bore on His body,[1] His death and resurrection.

> *And by His stripes we are healed. (Isaiah 53:5 NKJ)*

---

[1] Isaiah 53:5

Chapter Three

The Holy Spirit

Do you know that all the power you need to live a Godly life is found in the Holy Spirit? When Jesus physically left this earth, the one very important thing that He did was to send the Holy Spirit. The Holy Spirit is not only the third person of the trinity, but He was sent to us for a specific purpose. Before Jesus left He told His disciples:

> *But you will receive power when the Holy Spirit comes on you. (Acts 1:8a NIV)*

"What kind of power is that?" you might ask. Well, it is the genuine power of God. As the third person of the trinity, the Holy Spirit contains *all* of the attributes of God. He *is* God; not a part of God. Furthermore, when the Holy Spirit comes to live in us, that same power can be ours to exercise!

As I continued to grow in the Lord and my knowledge and experience expanded, so did the realization that there was even more that God had for me. I was still struggling with resentments and anger towards my husband and lingering insecurities;

however, greater than the desire for change was the desire for more of God. There it was, again, that deep hunger to know Him to a greater measure.

I didn't recognize exactly what I was asking for when I prayed, "God, I want all of you. I know there is more and I want more." Sometimes we don't need to have the knowledge or the insight in order to express our request. It comes as a stirring deep inside—a stirring to know God and experience all that He is and has for us.

It is difficult for me to describe other than to say, "I felt pulled along by God." At times you will hear me describe it as hunger or simply a desire for more, but it is really so much more than that. It is God drawing me to Himself because He *also* wants more. He wants to give me more of Himself and He wants more of *me*. This Bible verse explains it so well:

> *Eye has not seen, nor ear heard, nor have entered into the heart of man the things which God has prepared for those who love Him. But God has revealed them to us through His Spirit. For the Spirit searches all things, yes, the deep things of God. (I Corinthians 2:9–10 NKJ)*

At that time, I was so hungry that I was attending two different churches plus a mid-week prayer meeting. I must admit that some of my hunger was out of desperation. I was desperate for love and desperate for Jesus to change my life. Receiving Jesus had literally brought me from death to life. He awakened my deadened heart and gave me hope in the midst of a broken marriage. However, I knew that I needed more of His love and power to be healed of my emotional wounds.

I have discovered that I am a very tenacious individual. Now, sometimes that has worked against me, but in this circumstance it worked for me. Do you know that Jesus rewards our tenacity when it is focused on seeking Him?[2] Look at what Jesus said to His disciples:

> *Blessed are those who hunger and thirst for righteousness, for they will be filled. (Matthew 5:6 NIV)*

I am so thankful that in my searching Jesus put me in touch with the one woman who could point me in the direction I needed to go. It was at the break in the Sunday morning service when they serve donuts and coffee in the fellowship hall and I decided to go. I was standing alone when a woman came up to me and introduced herself as Joy. She looked about my age and, as we talked, her peaceful demeanor made me feel at ease with her. I mentioned that my prayer partner was on vacation and Joy offered to pray with me. We chatted a bit more and she gave me her phone number before we parted.

My life at home was still very challenging to me. Even though I had more hope since receiving the Lord, I still felt overwhelmed—sometimes on a daily bases. On one of my overwhelm days I called Joy. She assured me that she would be happy to pray with me and gave me her address so I could go and spend some time with her. On my drive there, I remember feeling a mixture of emotions. My desperation had reached an all time high; but there was also the Holy Spirit drawing me forward, which I recognized as an excitement that was building in my spirit.

Upon my arrival, Joy welcomed me with tea. I couldn't help but notice my anxiety poking to the surface, but Joy's smile and the ease with which she spoke helped calm me. She pointed to one of the two beautiful winged-back chairs framing her stone

---

[2] Luke 11:5–13

fireplace and invited me to sit as she sat in the adjacent chair facing me.

Joy asked, "Would you be comfortable if I opened our time with prayer?"

I said, "Of course."

She prayed, "Lord Jesus, would you come and be present in this time with us and give to Carol what you have for her today."

I noticed, right away, God's presence filling this space with her. I talked a little bit about my family and some of the stressors I was facing. Joy listened very intently and then asked, "Do you know the Holy Spirit?"

I knew the Holy Spirit was the third person of the trinity, but I didn't think that was what she implied in her question. Therefore, I said, "No, not really."

For the next hour she read to me scripture after scripture relating to the Holy Spirit from the New Testament. The scriptures spoke of the power to speak in other tongues,[3] the power to hear what the Spirit was saying,[4] the power to heal the sick and the power to deliver demons.[5] I was shocked, but my spirit was excited. I never thought that God could move in such miraculous ways. A statement that Joy kept saying over and over as she read was, "And God has this for you today." The final scripture she read to me was from the book of Acts:

> *And when Paul had laid hands on them, the Holy Spirit came upon them, and they spoke with tongues and prophesied. (Acts 19:6 NKJ)*

---

[3] Acts 2: 4
[4] Matthew 10: 20
[5] Matthew 10: 8

The moment that Joy read that scripture to me, I knew in my heart that I desired that experience. In fact, there was a sense deep inside me that this is what I had longed for all along.

I asked, "What must I do to receive this gift?"

She explained, "There really isn't anything to *do*. Just *ask and receive*."

She then led me in a simple prayer to Jesus asking Him for the infilling of the Holy Spirit. Joy put her hand on my head and began to pray in tongues. Her prayer was beautiful, but I didn't feel anything was happening to me. I was extremely disappointed. Joy explained, however, that sometimes people need to be alone with the Lord to receive what He has because they can be self-conscious of their reactions in front of someone else.

I was trying to take in her explanation, but as I drove home my head was full of negative self-talk. "Maybe the gift is not for me. Maybe I'm not good enough." Finally my prayer took over. "Lord Jesus, I really want all you have for me. I need your Holy Spirit." My heart continued to pour out my requests until I reached my home.

When at home, I went right into my prayer closet (which at the time was the bathroom), the only place I was guaranteed to be alone. I got on my knees and again poured out my heart to the Lord. I waited. My heart pounded wildly. I waited.

All of a sudden this liquid love poured through my body. That is the only picture I can think to give you, but that doesn't do justice to what I felt. The love of God is beyond description. I just know that I never felt that kind of love ever before. My body started to shake. With my hands raised I thanked God for His love over and over again until I felt a force, or something like a force, bubbling up inside of me. Out of my mouth popped a glorious heaven-sent language. Like a river, it kept flowing and flowing. Look, with me, at how Jesus describes this river:

> *Jesus stood and cried out, saying, 'If anyone thirsts, let him come to Me and drink. He who believes in Me, as the Scripture has said, out of his heart will flow rivers of living water.' But this He spoke concerning the Spirit, whom those believing in Him would receive. (John 7:37–39a NKJ)*

There I remained, saturated in that mystifying river for hours. My heart was being filled repeatedly and at the same time this new love was pouring out of my heart to Him—my Savior. I felt joined to Him and joined together with heaven. It was like an open heaven over me where I could reach in and touch God. There was no devision between us. At that moment there was no *heaven* and *earth*—there was just *unity*—I in Him and He in me. I was intensely aware that, given a choice, I never wanted to leave.

Eventually, I did get up and shifted from the bathroom to my bedroom. The Spirit directed me through an inner directive to my spirit to get my Bible and open it to Ezekiel 2:7. What happened next never happened again in my Christian life, although the impact of that message has followed me throughout my Christian life. As I opened the Bible to Ezekiel 2:7, the words on the page jumped out at me. The words, "You shall speak My words to them," were coming off the page in 3-D form. Wow! That is all I could say at the time.

I sat there examining and marveling at my message. I began to realize that this must be something I needed to pay attention to, even though I, presently, could not imagine what meaning it held for me. I wrote the reference down so I could go back and reflect on it. Much later, in my walk with the Lord, I came to realize that the message had to do with my gift of prophecy and speaking God's Word to others. I also teach and now write what I believe God wants me to say to others.

You may be questioning God's reasoning for giving me a message that I couldn't make sense of initially. However, what I now know to be true is that the *remembrance* of that experience is precisely what I need to encourage me to speak each time I doubt myself.

You see, God knows the end from the beginning. We live in linear time on earth, but God lives inside eternity where there is no beginning and no end. He knew that there would be times when I would doubt myself, my gift or God's Word and that I would need irrefutable assurance in that place. I do believe that a 3-D pop out message is pretty irrefutable.

It all started with a simple prayer for more of God. Although, this simple prayer led me on a spiritual quest, which landed me inside the *heart* of God—inside of His awesome, consuming, indescribable love. The infilling of His precious Holy Spirit was mystifying, but extremely satisfying. I was on my way towards learning how to live naturally in the supernatural.

And as you go, preach, saying, "The kingdom of heaven is at hand." (Matthew 10:7 NKJ)

Chapter Four

Jesus' Appearance

"Oh, my God!" shouted my husband, Tony.

It was Easter Sunday and his voice startled me out of my anxious state as I sat next to him for the first church service we had ever attended together in our married life. Nevertheless, I would have to wait a painful several weeks before discovering the *why* of what made Tony scream and the events leading up to that day.

During my season of growth in the Lord, the Holy Spirit was also working on my husband's heart—although, in his resistance against the Spirit, he was growing more and more agitated. The internal battle between Tony's fleshly desires and the Spirit was very evident. It reached a culmination the evening prior to Easter Sunday.

It started out like any other evening. We finished our dinner and the children were already in bed or in their rooms. Tony went to the refrigerator, grabbed a beer and turned on the TV. Normally, I would have gone into the bedroom to read my Bible and pray.

This evening, though, I decided I wanted to talk to him about our lack of communication and I turned off the TV. Tony said, "I don't want to talk right now" and turned the TV back on. I turned the TV back off. (I don't know what got into me, except maybe the Holy Spirit. You'll understand as this Easter story unfolds.)

Well, that punched my husband's buttons and he pushed me and stormed out of the house. I was stunned at Tony's explosion, but at the same time I was experiencing a lot of peace. I climbed into bed and decided to stay focused on the Lord by praying and reading the Word. In a short while, Tony came back in. He didn't share where he went and I didn't ask; however, he knelt down next to me, took my hand and asked my forgiveness for his anger. He also stated, "I decided to go to church with you tomorrow." This was not my husband! I knew God was working, but as yet, I didn't know quite how.

He didn't say another word until he got into bed. He tossed and turned a bit and moaned like he was in pain. I finally said, "What's the matter?" Tony said the bursitis in his hip was acting up. I felt led by God to ask, "Would you like me to pray for you?" And to my amazement he said, "Yes!"

I laid my hand on his hip and prayed out loud a very simple prayer for healing. I said, "Amen." And Tony said, "Amen." He thanked me and got up to use the restroom. Meanwhile, I was praying madly in my head, "God, would you touch my husband? Would you heal him? I want to believe. Help my unbelief." I know that wasn't exactly a prayer of faith—but that prayer was what I had to offer Him.

Tony came back to bed, but did not say anything else. I had a difficult time sleeping. My head was full of questions to the Lord. What was He doing? Was this God? I was stunned and confused. Don't you know that many times we are *stunned* and *confused* when God is moving.

The following morning there was the usual activity in preparation for attending church. I was making toast and eggs for the kids and I wasn't paying too much attention over the fact that Tony was not getting dressed. I thought, "Oh well, he is chickening out." I noticed that our daughter, Toni, said something to him and then he got up from the breakfast table and got ready for church.

I finished getting ready for church and tried to appear outwardly composed. Inwardly, I was shaking with excitement. My running dialog with the Lord was, "God, is this your timing? Would you meet my husband in the service." I remembered an arrow prayer I had shot to the Lord one day not too long ago, "Jesus, you know my husband only goes to church on Easter and Christmas, so if you don't get him now, you'll have to wait nine months." It was a silly prayer, but also really desperate—I sincerely didn't want to wait nine more months for things to change at home.

I still thought my husband might back out before getting in the car, but thankfully he did not. Except for the chatter from my children, it was a quiet drive to church. I don't know what Tony was thinking, but I was just trying to keep my nervous energy from erupting. Now that he was *really* in the car and *really* going to church, some of my fears began popping up, "What would he do with the speaking in tongues? Maybe since it is Easter, though, the pastor won't go there. I hope. And, what about the lifting of hands? I don't think he has ever experienced either."

A number of months ago, following my baptism of the Holy Spirit, the Lord led me to this little Foursquare Church down the street from the Baptist Church I was attending. I felt at home there from the minute I walked through the door and it lined up with where I was spiritually. However, now I was doubting my decision. Did I think my husband was going to find the Lord here, really? He had no positive background at all concerning pentecostalism. In fact, when young, he was taught to stay away from "those tongue speaking people."

As we walked into the sanctuary, I made a decision to give all of that to the Lord and trust Him. He had been faithful to lead me thus far and I had no reason to doubt Him now. I committed to giving myself to worship and leaving Tony to the Lord. I reminded myself that it would have to be God, by His Spirit, who would draw Tony to Himself—just as He had done with me.

I could never have imagined what Jesus was revealing to my husband and the heart change that was happening until weeks later when he broke his silence over it and began to share with me. It was a mind-boggling experience. You will see why he could not speak of it right away. Here is his story concerning the events which began the evening before Easter when he ran out of the house.

> *I was very confused and angry. I didn't know what was happening to my wife. I just know I didn't like it. I was mad at God for taking one wife from me (in death) and it felt like God was taking this wife from me. My anger took over and I pushed Carol. I ran out the door in my stocking feet and headed up New York Avenue.*
>
> *Out of the pitch darkness I heard a voice ask, "Tony, what are you doing?" I thought it might be my neighbor, Jack, messing with me. So, I asked, "Jack, is that you?" There was no answer. Then again I heard, "Tony!"*
>
> *Now I was mad. I responded, "Jack, stop screwing around with me. Where are you?" I started looking through the hedges to see if Jack was hiding there. There was NO Jack. Just then,*

an older gentleman was pushing the button to cross the street, so I asked him, "Did you say anything to me?" The man looked at me, crossed the street and vanished before my eyes.

Now I was scared, startled and wide awake. This time I heard, "Tony Romeo, this is the Lord your God." My only response was a plea. I shouted, "Don't kill me, God. Please don't kill me." It felt like the only thing that I could ask of God.

God assured me, "Tony, I am not going to kill you, but I want you to serve me. I want you to go home, apologize to your wife and go to church tomorrow with your family." (All of this conversation was with the audible voice of God.)

When I got home, my wife was in bed reading and there was a heavenly glow around her head. (The kind that you see in a picture around Jesus' or Mary's head.) I couldn't tell Carol what happened, but I did manage, "I'm sorry, honey. Will you forgive me? I'm going to go to church with you and the kids tomorrow, if that's OK with you?"

I climbed into bed with my hip hurting me a lot. I knew it was the bursitis acting up again. Carol asked if she could pray with me and I said, "Yes." I don't know what I expected; although, I know I got more than I imagined. When Carol put her hand on my hip, it felt like a red hot iron and the pain disappeared immediately. I needed to go to the bathroom and test my experience.

I started doing deep knee bends in the bathroom and found that there was yet another thing to confuse and amaze me—My hip did not hurt any more. I kept testing it out (bend up, bend up) with the same result. Did God use my wife to heal me? What was happening to me?

The next morning I awoke in still somewhat of a daze. I thought, "Was that a dream I had last night?" It was much too real, but on the other hand much too surreal. I decided to ignore it for now. I sat down at the breakfast table with my coffee. My daughter, Toni, was sitting there and she asked if I was going to church. I didn't know how to answer. Then, she reached out and touched my hand and said, "Daddy, the kids at church are asking me if I have a daddy." It wasn't her words, though, that startled me. Her hand felt as hot as my wife's hand the night before. I didn't know what all this meant, but I decided to go to church.

The church was small and a lot of people showed up for the service. The children went to children's church as Carol and I made our way into the sanctuary. I noticed that the people were more friendly than I had experienced years ago in church. They were hugging each other and chatting. Carol introduced me to several individuals. I was only concerned with getting in the pew and sitting down.

We ended up in the middle of the pew and more crammed than I would have liked. The service started and everyone stood to worship. I looked for a hymnal, but there wasn't any. The words to the songs were shown up on a screen. They had a band and the songs were very lively. A lot of people, including my wife were lifting their hands. This certainly was not the church I had remembered. My uneasiness was growing.

What happened next would change my life. Everyone including the pastor and including my wife began to sing in tongues. What I had heard about tongues was not good. So, I closed my eyes and prayed, "God, when I open my eyes would you show me the nearest exit so I can get the h—out of here."

When I opened my eyes, there was Jesus. He was standing behind the pastor (but much larger than the pastor) and he was looking at me. Jesus then pointed to me and said, "You, who are confused, this is my church and my people." That is when I screamed aloud, "Oh, my God!"

I don't remember the rest of the service. I wanted to exit as soon as possible when it was over. The pastor sped out another door and headed towards me in the parking lot. He had a big hug for me and said, "I hope you come to visit us again."

I didn't tell anyone about my vision. I needed some time to think about everything that had transpired. I was overwhelmed and still very much confused. Why would Jesus speak to me, heal my hip and appear to me? My sins were still very much on my mind.

The next several weeks felt like several months to me. As I stated before, Tony did not speak for the next number of weeks outside of directly answering a question. He was very subdued and pensive, which was a real turn about for my exuberant Italian husband. He did attend church with me during those several weeks, but did not give me a clue as to what God was doing.

One Wednesday evening he voiced that he wanted to go to church, but I wasn't feeling good and stayed at home. When he came home he was really excited. He told me, "I received the Lord tonight!" I was so excited and hugged him. I asked him to tell me all about it.

The pastor always gave an invitation at the end of his teaching for those people who wanted to receive Jesus to look up and he would pray for them. Well, Tony said that he was looking up for weeks, but the pastor never noticed him. That night, Tony had told God, "If he doesn't notice me tonight, I am never going back to that church." Well, he looked up and the pastor noticed him. He said, "Is that why you are looking at me, Tony?" Tony said, "Yes!" I found out later from the pastor that he thought Tony had looked up at him on Easter morning when Tony was looking at the open vision of Jesus.

When Tony finally shared with me all of the miracles Jesus had been doing in the space of several weeks, it might have been difficult for me to grasp, but remember, I had already been introduced to the amazing miraculous work of the Holy Spirit. My excitement was over-the-top indescribable—to think that I now could share this wondrous journey with my husband!

God's grace was certainly with us. We were heading down a very rocky trail without God. I was so thankful that I only had to wait two years for my husband to come to the Lord. Everything was not instantly fixed, but Jesus had revealed so much of Himself and so much of His love for us that we couldn't help returning that love to Him by serving Him and giving our lives to Him.

That Easter Sunday was the beginning of the life transformation that Jesus Christ would bring to our family. The wonders that God would unfold to us in the days, months and years ahead far surpassed the grandest expectations of my heart.

> *Great is the Lord! He is most worthy of praise! His greatness is beyond discovery! Let each generation tell its children of your mighty acts. I will meditate on your majestic, glorious splendor and your wonderful miracles… I will proclaim your greatness. (Psalm 145:3–6 NLT)*

Chapter Five

Jesus Heals our Addictions

Addictions are usually a form of escape. The root causes are the underlying emotional distresses that we are either unwilling to face and/or unable to face. We are emotional beings and that is a good thing. Our emotions help us to connect with each other and connect with God. Nevertheless, our emotions can become unruly and even destructive when we fail to process painful interactions or trauma and relegate those wounded emotions to an underground habitat in our psyche.

If left unattended, the defense mechanisms, which are holding those emotions in check, start to break down and the unwarranted emotions start to make their way to the surface. We are faced with a choice at that point to either deal with these emotions in a healthy manner or avoid them. Sadly, if we haven't been taught any other way, we avoid them. Addictions, of all sorts, are often used to aid the numbing process.

As I shared earlier, Tony and I both had numerous addictions before receiving the Lord. Alcohol addiction and long-term nicotine use was passed down in both of our families. Violence was another familial addiction, one that required the most attention to conquer. (I will talk more about that later.) Anger and sadness fueled both of our addictions resulting from the unhealed wounds of past relationships. For Tony, it was the wounds surrounding his failed marriage and mine were mainly childhood wounds. We both brought into our marriage these unhealed past wounds and never realized the destruction it could bring—not only to one another, but also to our children.

Our alcohol use had progressed from parties, special occasions and socializing to an everyday occurrence. As my sadness in my marriage grew, so also did my drinking. I would start mixing margaritas in mid afternoon just to make it through my overwhelming day. Tony drank mostly beer in the evening but frequented the bars several times a week where he drank hard liquor.

After I received the Lord, I remember asking the Lord, "Do you want me to give this up and, if so, when?" It was not that God gave me a clear directive—He simply took away the desire. And, I never relapsed back into it. Before my husband was converted, I would go to the bar with him and drink cola. I can recall how stunned he was.

After Tony's conversion, he asked me the same question, "When does God show you to quit drinking?" I told him, "Don't worry, he'll show you." Well, he went to the bar one more time and never went again. Jesus did the same thing for him; He simply took the desire away.

Now, I realize that there may be many addicts reading this who would want the same kind of experience. I consider Tony's and my deliverance from alcohol to be miraculous. There was nothing we had to do to achieve freedom except desire to follow God's ways. It is OK to seek a miracle, but it is not the only way God moves.

Some of my expertise as a counselor is in the area of substance abuse recovery. In that role, I do pray for individuals. Although, I also send them to twelve step groups and instruct them in the various methods of healing. I remind you, God still reserves the right to be God and move in the way He deems appropriate.

I believe that Jesus is a miracle working God. I believe healing is part of what He purchased for us on the cross. I believe we should go to Him and ask in faith. I believe that He is a loving gracious God. However, He does not always act in the same way. That is where trust is developed. We need to believe more in His character—loving, faithful, kind, generous, good, benevolent, forgiving and trustworthy—than in fulfilled or unfulfilled expectations!

The journey of becoming more like Christ is just that—a journey. It is a process through which we come to know Jesus and His love to a greater extent. And inside the safety of His love, He begins to show us those areas He wants to change. This transformation process can look different for each individual. Jesus knows what each of us needs in order for growth to take place.

I love the miraculous transformations. Most often miracles impact an individual in such a profound way that it produces a *life* transformation—a totally different way of viewing and responding to one's life. But, what you will see as I continue to tell my story is that God sometimes withholds the miraculous for the opportunity to teach the individual in a different manner. Let me show you the differing ways that God delivered both Tony and I from our nicotine addictions. Here is Tony's story:

> Shortly after I made Jesus my Lord, I felt like He wanted me to stop smoking. I prayed and made that commitment to Him. There I was, the first day and I was a wreck! I went to sleep that night and dreamt that I was putting

ketchup on a bowl of cigarettes and eating them. When I woke up, I said to myself and God, "I can't do this." My wife suggested I call my pastor.

Pastor Ron picked up the phone right away and said, "Praise God!" when I told him that I decided to give up smoking. I said, "Wait a minute. Don't praise God too soon. I can't do it." I told him about my dream and I told him I was a wreck.

The pastor told me that wasn't a problem. He said, "When you get off the phone, lift up your hands to God and ask Him to give you the power and He will."

I did what he said and right there in the middle of my TV shop, I felt this warm liquid sensation go through my body. It flooded my whole body and when it left, all the anxiousness was gone. I never felt the need for another cigarette and my body was completely freed of any withdrawal symptoms.

Now, let's look at my story: I never smoked another cigarette from the day that I gave my addiction to the Lord. However, I wore out my knees in prayer, praying for deliverance from nicotine. I still had a desire to smoke after one year (though I resisted the desire.) At the time, it really annoyed me that my husband was completely delivered and my deliverance seemed to be an agonizing ritual. The reality is, though, as I look back at the experience, my relationship with the Lord grew tremendously during that year and now I can say, "I wouldn't want it any other way."

These are the times when we have to trust the goodness and the *wisdom* of God. We can't always see, in the middle of a struggle, what is really the best way. In my struggle over nicotine

I had to keep going back to the Lord, laying my need before Him and trusting that it was in His hands. But, what I didn't recognize at the time, was that it was building my faith bit by bit. Here is how the Bible describes the process:

> *Let us strip off every weight that slows us down, especially the sin that so easily hinders our progress. And let us run with endurance the race that God has set before us. We do this by keeping our eyes on Jesus, on whom our faith depends from start to finish.* (Hebrews 12:1b–2a NLT)

Therefore, Jesus is always inside the process with us. Whether we receive from Him the instantaneous miracle, or we receive day by day the strength to overcome our failings, Jesus is forever by our side.

Anger and rage was another area where Tony and I needed the power of God to overcome the behavior. Anger and our reaction to it—violence—can become an addictive behavior, especially if we have been raised in a household where violent outbursts were the norm for dealing with angry feelings. (Both Tony and I experienced that in our respective childhood homes.)

My anger did not blossom until I was ushered into the role of caring for four children largely without the help of my husband. I think there would have been any number of circumstances, however, that would have caused my anger to surface since the pattern had already been learned in my family of origin. My husband, also, was becoming increasingly more violent and together our anger was erupting on each other and onto the children.

I allowed resentments to build towards my husband to the point where any number of his behaviors or verbal communications could trigger me. I was feeling increasingly out of control, which also escalated my abusive behavior towards my children. The last thing I wanted to do was hurt my children the way I was hurt. Now, in our rational mind we think that that desire would be enough to stop the behavior, but we are talking about an addictive behavior that gains strength each time it is acted out. It was a vicious cycle that I didn't know how to gain freedom from.

In my turmoil, I picked up a book written by a Christian author, Stormie Omartian called *Stormie*. She shared about her own struggles with anger and how she, together with the Lord, found solutions. I took her advice and it worked! Every time I felt my anger rising in me, I told my children, "Mommy is going to do a time-out and we will talk about your discipline later."

I would then go to my bedroom, shut the door and pray until the rage left my body and I was more clear headed. Afterwards, I could discipline my children from a rational place. As for my husband and I, we decided together that if we started heading into a heated argument, we would stop and pray. These new behaviors required work (a lot of work), but the Holy Spirit was faithful to meet us there and eventually our violent outbursts stopped. I can't tell you that it was an overnight battle. Those behaviors were deeply engrained in both of us.

When I look at Tony's story and mine, I am so thankful that Jesus gave us another chance. But, it wasn't just another chance. God didn't say, "OK, pick yourselves up and try again." No, He came and picked us up and not only opened our blind eyes to see Him (which was marvelous), but He infused us with a *power* to be different, transformed, new, changed, altered, our lives fixed on Him.

My encouragement to you is, "Don't give up." If you find that your journey into freedom is lengthy, please don't lose sight of the bigger picture. The bigger picture is that God is bigger and He won't give up. Even when we might fail, He doesn't give up on us. Tony and I experienced many failings in our process, but we just kept going and just kept believing in our Big God.

> *Being confident of this very thing, that He who has begun a good work in you will complete it until the day of Jesus Christ. (Philippians 1:6 NKJ)*

Chapter Six

Angelic Protection

Angels are curious beings. They are probably so fascinating to us because they are so totally supernatural. We are drawn to this otherworldliness about them. Sometimes we forget, however, that even though we usually can't see them, they are with us everyday helping and encouraging us. Here is what God promises in His Word:

> *If you make the Lord your refuge, if you make the Most High your shelter, no evil will conquer you; no plague will come near your dwelling. For he orders his angels to protect you wherever you go. They will hold you with their hands to keep you from striking your foot on a stone. (Psalm 91:9–12 NLT)*

Many times we can see the work of angels without really seeing them; nevertheless, there are times that the Lord pulls back the veil and allows us to view these majestic creatures. Here are several occasions the Lord did this for Tony and I.

After several life-changing years with the Lord, I noticed my health was beginning to fail. I was a dancer and I owned my own dance studio where I taught daily. The first thing that I began to notice was an increasing level of fatigue. I always had good energy, but I brushed off the idea that anything was wrong and attributed the fatigue to the fact that I was now teaching and taking care of house and children.

Time passed and I began to notice pain in my muscles and pain and stiffness in my joints. It felt like I had just overworked them and so I started soaking in a hot tub and stretching more. Nothing seemed to help. In fact, it continued to worsen. As my illness continued, my physical activity became more and more limited. Finally, I could barely care for my small children as my only physical movement was from the bed to the couch and back to the bed again.

This was a particularly scary time for me. I started going from one doctor to the next in the hopes of gaining some answers. (It wasn't till years later that I received a diagnosis of fibromyalgia and received some treatment that was successful in aiding my daily function.) It felt like my body was betraying me. I had spent my whole life, up until this time, dancing. I counted on my vibrant physical condition. I couldn't envision a different life. My emotions were already strained because of my strained marriage and now my physical pain, and confusion over its' origins, compounded my deteriorating emotional state.

I felt lost. After having experienced such miraculous high times with the Lord, this was a plummet that sent me down to the depths within. I continued to get prayer every time it was offered at church, although I was becoming increasingly more withdrawn. I was tired of requesting prayer for my condition and even more tired of other's insensitive comments regarding my illness. I was aware that Jesus is a supernatural God who had already miraculously healed me once (Chapter Two); nonetheless, that experience felt so far away and my faith was waning.

In the midst of my suffering, I also became afflicted with hives all over my body. I went through several months of treatment with no success. Many nights, in the middle of the night, I would drag myself into the shower to try and soothe the unbearable pain from the welts that covered my flesh. It was also the one place that I could weep without disturbing the family. I reached the end of my coping skills, though, and one night I woke my husband to drive me to the hospital.

The hospital experience itself was horrific. When the nurses did manage to get an IV drip in me (after 2 hours of trying to find a vein) that was the *only* treatment I received for 36 hours. I was told not to get out of bed and the nurses were nasty to me because they were tired of my complaining. I was given no medication—not even aspirin. No doctors showed up and I didn't have a phone in my room to call anyone. I felt trapped, but I didn't have the strength to do anything about it.

A young nurse came into the room to change the IV fluid. She had left the room already when I noticed an air bubble at least 3–4 inches long travel into the tube in my arm. I started ringing the buzzer for the nurse, but of course there was no response. I could then feel the bubble as it made its way through the veins in my body. I was starting to panic. It was then that I saw (by the Spirit) four dark angels at the four corners of my bed.

Satan had been lying to me throughout my hospital ordeal that he was going to kill me. I was able to pray and shake off his lies until this moment. Nevertheless, in my weakness and confusion, I managed to say aloud, "Jesus." In that instant, the dark angels disappeared and were replaced with four bright angels of light. With their wings opened, they covered my bed like a canopy. I knew in my spirit that I was not going to die. I would soon discover that I also needed that certainty to survive an experience I would have the following day.

I slept well in the peace of God and when I woke up I had the strength to ask for a phone and called my husband. I simply told him, "Get me out of this hospital." He called my doctor to find out what was going on and my doctor finally arrived at the hospital. He was there about five minutes when I went into anaphylactic shock. I've never experienced anything so scary. My lungs collapsed, I couldn't breathe and had severe pain in my heart.

They did not have oxygen on the unit, so they had to wheel my bed down the hall, into the elevator and down to the intensive care unit. Through my fear, though, I remembered my angelic companions and the guarantee from God that I was not going to die, and then I lost consciousness.

God will often open our spiritual eyes and give us visions when he is trying to give us knowledge about the situation. This can move us to pray, act or simply receive His assurance. In my situation, I was moved by the Holy Spirit to speak the name of Jesus against the enemy and I also received His assurance that reduced my fear of dying. When I talk about *seeing*—let me describe the different ways that we can *see*. I more often see in my mind's eye. It is like the picture is inside my mind. Or, I could say that it is my spirit that is seeing what is there. Now, there are times that people see physically what is there or they may sense the presence of angelic beings. All of these ways are governed and gifted by the Holy Spirit.

The ability to *see* is miraculous or supernatural because it is an experience that is initiated by God with the intention of bringing His transforming power into our circumstance and to our thinking. He gives us *a vision to change our current vision*. In my hospital bed, I was only seeing through the eyes of fear and powerlessness. Jesus wanted me to know that He was still in charge and would protect me. That angelic vision was successful in encouraging me in that traumatic moment, and its remembrance has continued to impact me throughout my walk with my God.

The memory centers of our brain are extraordinary. One thing science has discovered about memory is that we have a better chance of remembering the events that impact us the most—positively or negatively. I believe that is why supernatural experiences are remembered with great detail many years after the event. What science can't prove, however, is the way those experiences *impact* our *spirit*. The miraculous becomes imprinted not only in our brains, but also in our spirits, because we are spiritual beings; not just physical ones.

Let me back up and visit my near-death experience once again. There was no doubt in my mind that Jesus had rescued me from the hand of the enemy. Although I did not possess any way of mentally processing just what happened to me, I just knew. When I regained consciousness, a nurse was holding my hand. My space inside the ICU was silent outside of the myriad of beeping sounds that attested to the fact that I was indeed still alive.

The next person I saw was a doctor I had not met before who stated that he was an allergist specialist and that he was treating me with IV steroids. The only question I asked was, "Am I going to get well?" He assured me that the steroids would reduce the inflammation and he would watch my response to the medication. He asked if I had any more questions, but I couldn't pull my thoughts back from wherever they went. The only response I was left with was a blank stare. He returned the stare and then left without another word.

When I dared to look at my internal state, I noticed that my mind felt as sterile as the room I was in. The crisis left my psyche in a kind-of disconnected state. I had this strange feeling of emptiness like I didn't know where I belonged. I don't know if that was a shock reaction to the crisis itself or from being yanked back from death.

In the following days leading to my recovery, the Holy Spirit prayed through me continually. Sometimes I prayed in tongues, but more often I just knew the Spirit was praying. What amazed me the most, though, was when the Spirit spoke into my mind all the words that He was praying. It was so comforting and encouraging to actually hear His prayers. I could feel my spirit and soul being filled up with Spirit's loving words. They were nourishment for my soul.

The Spirit spoke to me about building me up on the inside. He spoke to me consistently about the restoration work that He was doing—that the very thing, which now looks like it is in ruins, will be beautiful and will bring glory to God. Furthermore, that I would have joy instead of mourning, beauty out of ashes and a garment of praise in place of the spirit of heaviness.[6]

The grace of God then met me in another miraculous way. I was visited by the felt presence of God—which I later came to call my "bubble of God." I could sense in my spirit as well as in my body that this presence was three feet deep and completely surrounded my body. It was in essence a bubble surrounding me. And, it was a substance. It wasn't just a vision of God's presence. It *was* God's presence.

Above all, His presence felt protective. I *knew* that nothing of the enemy would harm me, neither spiritual nor physical. I didn't just believe, I *knew*. I felt so deeply cared about and cared for. It was more than love—at least how I usually think of love. To feel surrounded by and protected by the God that created the universe is an awesome experience. I could rest, not in a superficial way, but a deep rest of the soul.

I realize now, as I look back, that I was in grave need of that deep rest. My emotional being had been breaking down, along with my physical, and for the healing that I needed, I would have to relax fully into the arms of my God. This experience lasted a total of three months. During that time, His felt presence never lifted.

---

[6] Isaiah 61:3–4

> *Those who live in the shelter of the Most High will find rest in the shadow of the Almighty… He will shield you with his wings. He will shelter you with his feathers. His faithful promises are your armor and protection. (Psalm 91:1, 4 NLT)*

I was not the only one that Satan was lying to regarding my physical state. Tony was also hearing, "I am going to take your wife from you. She is not going to live!" These lies were somewhat abated when I did recover and was sent home, but since my health was uncertain, the enemy could still get his hook into Tony's mind.

After I had been at home for several weeks, Tony was awakened in the middle of the night. This is what he related to me the next day:

> *When I first woke up, I didn't realize why I was awake. Then I recognized light coming from the opened door to the bedroom. I had to focus my eyes a bit because the light was bright. I wanted to wake up my wife, but I heard the Lord say, "No, let her sleep."*
>
> *What I noticed next was that the light formed into two columns or figures of light. The figures did not have any features. They looked more like smoky columns with the light shinning out from within them. I asked the Lord what I was seeing. He said, "They are my angels."*
>
> *I watched as one of the angels moved from the doorway, came around to my wife's side of the bed and positioned itself over her body. It stayed over her for several minutes. Then it*

> moved back to the doorway, joined the other angel and they both disappeared.
>
> I couldn't wait to talk to Carol the next morning. I was sure the angel came with healing power for her. When she woke up, the first thing I asked her was, "How do you feel?" When she responded that she was in pain, my first reaction was disappointment. I know what I saw was miraculous and I felt that she was miraculously healed.
>
> I still feel the angel came with healing power for her even though she was not instantaneously healed. The experience did boost my faith and my ability to pray for healing for my wife. I was sure, in my heart, that Jesus had healing for her and was protecting her. The lies the enemy was feeding me, that she would die, were broken.

This is what excites me so much regarding miracles. They not only reveal the power of God to us, but the experience itself comes with a message that speaks to our point of need. Tony's experience with the angels infused him with hope and faith for my recovery and broke Satan's lie. It was a faith changing moment.

The other thing I would like you to notice about miracles is that they are varied.

Our God is a creative God. He not only knows exactly what we need—but He also has the creative power to meet that need. That combination is awesome and powerful. Try and stretch your thinking a bit. Here is this being—God—who has the power to create in infinite ways. He never runs out of new ideas. He has an imagination that is limitless.

Now, expand that image to include a Being who is all knowing and all loving. He can speak and create into our situation the exact miracle that can bring us hope, vision, transformation, healing, faith, motivation, a changed heart, vitality, passion—whatever we need. That is more than exciting! I don't know about you, but my mind sometimes has a hard time taking that in.

This brings me to my next thought about miracles. We can sometimes get caught up in the experience and miss the message that God wanted to impart to us. The very nature of the supernatural can excite and distract us. We can get caught up in the WOW…this is wonderful…this is God…and forget to pay attention to what God is saying or doing.

Look, again, at my husband's experience. Because he interpreted the angelic visitation as a spontaneous healing for me, his initial response (when I wasn't healed) was disappointment. He had to reflect on it awhile before he could recognize the hope God was imparting to him. We both later realized, as well, that God *was* imparting healing to me, even though it was not a spontaneous healing.

> *But as it is written: "Eye has not seen, nor ear heard, nor have entered into the heart of man the things which God has prepared for those who love Him."[7] But God has revealed them to us through His Spirit. For the Spirit searches all things, yes, the deep things of God. (I Corinthians 2:9–10 NKJ)*

---

[7] Isaiah 64:4

Chapter Seven

Deliverance

Another type of miracle is the miracle of deliverance from the demonic. Even though the topic is controversial, I must talk about it here because deliverance was such a necessary part of my healing.

I believe avoidance of the deliverance ministry comes from confusion in the church over the role of Satan and demons in our lives. There is a portion of believers who would rather not pay attention to the enemy because they believe that doing so would give Satan more power. There is another portion of believers who pay too much attention to the demonic and place the blame for their unrighteous behaviors on Satan. Both of these extremes come out of ignorance.

This is how I understand the demonic and our battle between good and evil. Let's look firstly at the role that Satan fills. His name was Lucifer and he was a high-ranking angel among the host of heavenly angels. His evil desires began when he pursued his longing to *be* God. A battle ensued and God cast him out of heaven to abide on the earth. A third of the angels, who joined Lucifer and his intentions, were cast out of heaven to the earth as well. I believe that it is the fallen angels that we refer to as demons. There are other theories on the origins of demons, but that is my understanding.

One thing that is very important to remember is that God and Satan are not rivals. They are not equal in power. Satan is a created being and not the Creator. He can exert some power over us, but he is not all powerful. He also cannot be everywhere at the same time—omnipresent. Only God is omnipresent. Therefore, he uses his demons to do his work of taunting and belittling us and persuading us to turn from Jesus Christ. Most of his work transpires in our mind, will and emotions. Nevertheless, he does also have the power to sicken us in body as well. I believe the hives that I suffered from were a direct result of demonic influence.

Our will is of ultimate importance in fighting Satan and the demonic. Sometimes we want to blame the enemy for our problems when it is our weak will that is to blame. Just as it takes a decision of the will to receive the Lord, it takes a decision of the will to keep focused on that goal and not turn away. Sin (especially habitual sin) is one thing that opens the door for the enemy. Demons can also gain influence through sickness (notably mental illness) and trauma (when someone else sins against us.) Most of the time, even when demons gain entrance into the body, the person is not possessed. Possession denotes complete control over the individual and that is very rare. I believe it is because Jesus is faithful to protect our hearts. I have heard testimonies of people deeply involved in Satanic worship and yet they still gained the ability to turn their hearts to God.

Most of the time, I use the term demonized—which means, the person is being influenced by demons either internally or externally. It is not really important to find out exactly where the demon is. We just need to focus on what changes need to happen in the will to weaken the demon's power.

My first recognition of the demonic came through my personal experience. I had not as yet been taught concerning the demonic, but I learned through first hand experience. I shared, earlier, how the enemy had taunted me with the lie, "I am going to kill you." Actually, that lie was coming straight from the demon that was living in me. It wasn't Satan just placing that thought in my mind, the voice was coming from inside. At times there was more than one voice taunting, but the main rhetoric was, "WE are going to kill you."

The demons also caused me internal pain. The pain became so severe in my head that some nights I would literally run the streets to try and distract myself from the agony. It was very clear to me that it was the demonic that was assaulting me. I wasn't afraid. I just wanted to figure out how to get free. That consumed most of my prayers at that time.

I didn't know who I could confide in concerning my battle with the enemy. My husband was a new Christian and I was afraid he would react adversely. This was my first experience with the demonic. I had not read any scripture regarding the experience, so I did not know what my pastor would even say. I was finally pushed to confide in someone, however, because the pain and my desperation to find an answer was increasing.

I decided to tell my pastor, who responded by saying, "The elders and I are praying for you." That sure didn't feel like enough. I was pleading with God for answers. I was so afraid no one could help. At the same time, I was getting sicker in my body. The body pain was increasing and, as I revealed earlier, I began breaking out in hives all over my body. I never did receive any direct help or answers from the pastor at that time because I signed myself into the hospital to get the medical attention I needed, which was another futile attempt at wellness.

When I was released from the hospital, the hives had at least been cured, but, I realized that my mind was so disordered that I was not sure I could function in a rational way and care for my children. I felt very fragile in my body and mind. I did have my God bubble around me, though, and strangely I knew I would be all right (even though I didn't have a clue how.) The clear understanding I had had concerning the demonic (prior to the hospital stay) was not as present. My mind had now turned into a scrambled mush. That is the only way to describe it.

Again, I related my dilemma to my pastor and he suggested I come in and we would talk about it. I had decided that I was going to ask him for referrals to a mental health facility. My mind had become so confused, I couldn't grasp another solution. When I went in for my appointment, though, Pastor Ron focused back on the demonic. He handed me a book called *Deliver Me From Evil* by Don Basham and instructed me to read it before my next session. He said he would set up another appointment, together with a female elder in the church, to pray for deliverance for me. I wasn't sure that would work, but I did gain a level of expectancy.

That week, I devoured the book. I found myself on every page and gained some hope that Jesus was going to set me free. I recognized that the stories Don told in his book were "my story." He possessed the knowledge to adequately describe what was happening and how to gain freedom. As I read, I was relieved. I now had an explanation that came with a solution.

I also began reading *Pigs in the Parlor* by Frank and Ida Mae Hammond and through it began to realize some of the reasons I was so demonized. They write:

> *Evil spirits have no sense of fairness. They never hesitate to take full advantage of times of weakness in a person's life. Of course the weakest time in most lives is childhood. A child is completely dependent upon others for protection. Without question the majority of demons encountered through ministry have entered persons during childhood… How often I have heard replies such as, "My father was an alcoholic." They go on to relate various fears*

associated with this condition in the home. There was insecurity and often poverty because their father was unable to provide, or spent the family income in support of his addiction. As a child in such a home grows a little older he becomes embarrassed and ashamed.

Although I could then see how my childhood contributed to my emotional distress and demonization, it wasn't until years later, while in therapy, that I understood more fully the psychological ramifications. Of course, the foundational cause was the trauma to my psyche due to the violence and neglect.

When I returned for my appointment with Pastor Ron, God was gracious to deliver me. In fact, I had a number of appointments where Jesus, by His Spirit, set me free. Deliverance is a miraculous experience. I not only could feel the release of demons from my body, but the greater part of my experience was the power of God I felt come over me and move through me.

At times, I shook under the power. Sometimes, I could feel the river of His love washing and cleansing my soul as I cried tears of release and joy. There were times that I screamed. But, always, always, always there was the tenderness of His Spirit present—caring for me and tending my heart.

It was a very awesome encounter with Jesus, the One who paid the price for my deliverance at the cross. My heart was so full of gratitude. I couldn't stop praising my God. I knew that this washing and cleansing came from Him because He longed to create in me a new person. I *knew* I belonged to Him. I was His child. I had entered into a new world with Him—the Kingdom of God had come to earth through me.

After my first deliverance, I experienced an instantaneous release from the head pain and the voices. And, after every session, there was always greater clarity in my mind, more peace in my spirit and more healing in my emotions and body. I can state with great assurance, "Every deliverance was miraculous." I wouldn't be a functional person today without God's supernatural interventions.

There was another process that I had to actively engage in, however. That process was learning how to replace the enemy's lies with the truth from God's Word.

Deliverance is casting out the negative influence, but we need to be able to replace it with positive affirmation. And, the best positive affirmation is what God has to say to us, about us.

During my season of healing, I played Bible tapes almost continually. I spent time in prayer examining my heart and allowing the Holy Spirit access to it. I had index cards with scriptural truth written on them that I carried with me wherever I went. In the moments when I was assaulted with confusion or lies, I had to stop whatever I was doing and read and repeat God's promises.

Most of my deliverance took place over a three month period. Amazingly, but not a coincidence, my God bubble lasted three months. That is an example of God's attention to detail. He knew exactly what I needed to be able to withstand the deep healing that He would bring to me.

The bulk of my deliverance was instantaneous and miraculous. Nevertheless, what I would like you to understand is that deliverance is *always* happening as we align ourselves to God's ways. It is our will and the decisions we make concerning our relationship with the Lord which determines if we are walking a path of righteousness or opening ourselves up to the deviousness of Satan. Here is what scripture tells us:

Therefore submit to God. Resist the devil and he will flee from you. (James 4:7 NKJ)

When we are looking to God daily, being filled with His truth, being filled with His Spirit, being filled with righteousness, there is no place for the enemy. Satan and the demonic cannot dwell in the same place with righteousness. This is the truth of who we are in Christ:

> *For you were once darkness, but now you are light in the Lord. Walk as children of light (for the fruit of the Spirit is in all goodness, righteousness, and truth), finding out what is acceptable to the Lord. And have no fellowship with the unfruitful works of darkness, but rather expose them. (Ephesians 5:8–11 NKJ)*

I discovered that the Holy Spirit is very skilled at that job—exposing our unrighteousness and exposing the works of the enemy. Our job is to be alerted to the Holy Spirit and alerted to the ways of the enemy.[8] We are told to persevere in our faith.[9]

That vigilance is what needs to happen if we are to be made into the image of Christ. Our faults need to be exposed and we need to gain the muscle to walk a walk of faith.

One last note about the ministry of deliverance. Demons are not to become our focus, either out of fear or pride ("Look how the demons obey me."[10]) Jesus Christ is always in control and He *is* the Deliverer. Therefore, our eyes should always be focused on Jesus.

> *And let us run with endurance the race that is set before us, **looking** unto Jesus, the author and finisher of our faith. (Hebrews 12:1b–2a NKJ)*

---

[8] 1 Peter 5:8
[9] Hebrews 12:1
[10] Luke 10: 20

Chapter Eight

Healing of the Heart

This next season of my journey led me into the secret places of my heart. Through my deliverances there were many walled-off places of my heart that were now opened to the creative work of the Spirit. The first thing that happened in the process, however, was that all the dark feelings that had been housed beneath a closed door began to surface.

The childhood that I thought was good was now appearing painfully cold. I didn't know how this could be, but I had too many awesome experiences with God not to trust Him now in yet another layer of my healing. A deep sense of abandonment, grief, hopelessness, fear and sadness was being uncovered. I began to have dreams of being trapped inside empty scary houses in which I couldn't discover a way out. I would wake with my soul flooded with the sickened emotions. Sometimes, I just lay frozen in fear in my bed and unable to move. I wanted to speak the name of Jesus to see if He would lift this paralyzing terror, but I found I couldn't speak.

After an hour or so, when I could finally move, I forced my body to the living room. I had a plaque on my coffee table that contained the 23rd Psalm. I found it was comforting to read it out-loud until the bulk of my fear lifted. I don't remember how many months I was trapped in this crazed behavior, but during that time, I came to recognize some of the trauma hidden within.

This is when I began to discover just how split my psyche was. There was the personality I functioned in through most of my childhood and young adulthood. That personality was basically a smiling happy looking child. I had recognized from very young that this child was the one my mother wanted and so I had learned to please her. The pain, nevertheless, was still present, but buried under walls of denial and protection.

My parents divorced right after my first birthday. My father was an alcoholic who was extremely violent and beat my mother. My mom and I went to live with her parents for the next four years until my mother remarried. Sadly, husband number two also became an alcoholic and eventually violent as well. My mom soon became the co-alcoholic and their lives became structured around their addictions.

I was left alone on Friday and Saturday nights, so they could go to the bar and drink until 3 AM. They usually came home in a drunken rage at one another and I would be a witness, from my up-stairs bedroom, to the shouting, swearing, slamming doors and sometimes hitting. The fear kept me glued to the bed for hours. We only had a downstairs bathroom and I remember having to urinate so badly, but I could not get out of bed and go down the stairs. I had to wait, sometimes hours, before everything got quiet and it felt safe enough to go down.

My mother also started working after my eighth birthday and so I was a typical latch-key kid. I was responsible to wake by an alarm, make my breakfast, get dressed and arrive to school on time. Going home was not much brighter. My stepdad either arrived home from work mid-day, downed a couple of beers and passed out or he went to the bar and didn't come home till dinner quite drunk. In the midst of this chaos, he also sexually abused me. I had no one to turn to. I missed my grandmother tremendously, as she was the one person I was attached to, and my grandparents had moved away about this same time.

There are so many details I could add, but I think you can get the picture that my childhood was anything but happy. My training as a therapist has now taught me that a split can occur in the personality when a young child is traumatized. It is like the psyche itself says, "This distress is too much for this person to deal with. So, we are going to split off the pain so the psyche can remain whole."

Therefore, the happy child can continue to go to school and function, while the bulk of the pain is relegated to the split-off part of the personality. This is a very simplistic explanation of a disorder called DID or Dissociative Identity Disorder. Here is a good definition from the book, *Dissociative Identity Disorder:*

> *The dissociative identity disorders patients…suffer from an overwhelming loss of self and identity formation. Dissociation functions as a silent defense against overwhelming trauma, but contributes to a disintegration of development.*

As I learned about my own DID, I began by noticing the hidden pain when the walls or the defenses of my psyche began to come down. The Holy Spirit is an expert at transformation. Acting in trust, I continued to give myself, wholly, to the Lord.

My deepest desire was that He would own my heart. I just didn't realize, for Him to accomplish that task, He had to dismantle the structure that kept Him from bringing healing into those pain places.

Deliverance had done it's work, but I now had to allow the Holy Spirit to complete that work. This is the scripture I clung to during that time:

> *For God has not given us a spirit of fear and timidity, but of power, love, and self-discipline. (2 Timothy 1:7 NLT)*

The Holy Spirit was very faithful to His promises to heal me; however, this part of my healing process was very slow. Deliverance of a demon can be instantaneous, but the healing of the psyche and emotions can become lengthy and laborious. It is still a supernatural wonder, nevertheless—us working together with God Himself to see a marvelous transformation of the soul. That is the miracle we have to keep in our minds when we are going through the painful process of mending the soul.

During my heart-rending process, Jesus was faithful to give me some blueprints of what He was doing. Those details gave me the courage to keep moving forward and not slide back into the despair. I have said this before, "Jesus knows exactly what we have need of and He is so willing to meet us." At times, though, we have to listen closely because He may be speaking in that still small voice that is hard to hear. We also need to be looking *towards* Him for the encouragement. If we are looking the other way, distracted by our distress, we may miss His words of care and strength.

The Holy Spirit spoke to me frequently during that time. I journaled my prayers to God as well as His responses to me.

Many of my poems and meditations are included in my book, *Meditations from the River*. Here is one example from the book:

Wait For the Morning

I gazed at my reflected image
Tears and stains, brokenness and pain
Was all I could envision.

Where was the beauty I was destined for?
Was this God's final creation?
Certainly He held a greater plan for my life.

"I have a better plan—a plan of redemption.
It is not over yet. My resurrection life
Is at work in you.

"I conquered the grave. It didn't end there.
That was not the final work.
The greater work came in the morning."

Will you wait for the morning?
If it is evening and you are in the tomb,
Will you wait for the morning?

(p. 35)

The tomb is not a fun place to be in! There were times when I felt death all around me—death of my dreams, desires, hope, joy. But God was right there with me. My heart's cry was always, "Yes, Lord, I will wait," even when my flesh was screaming, "No!" The healing process wasn't always beautiful as I was going through it, but the Holy Spirit uncovered places along the way where I caught glimpses of the beauty that God was bringing to me.

One picture I saw, while meditating, was of a beautiful crystal vase. Jesus was holding it up and admiring it. I asked of Him the meaning. Jesus said, "This crystal vase represents you. It is clear and transparent so that my glory can shine through it. I am taking you on a difficult path of cleansing the flesh because I need *my character* to shine through you, not your own. I see the finished product and it is beautiful."

It is so easy for us to forget that that is what our walk with the Lord is all about—His character transforming ours.

> *Beloved, now we are children of God; and it has not yet been revealed what we shall be, but we know that when He is revealed, we shall be like Him, for we shall see Him as He is. And everyone who has this hope in Him purifies himself, just as He is* **pure.** *(I John 3:2–3 NKJ)*

The truth is, the more deeply we allow the Holy Spirit in to heal our soul, the more we become intimately entwined with the very essence of Jesus Christ. *This is* the hope that lives in us. We are not just getting our characters changed. (We might be able to gain some of that through self-help classes.) We are becoming *one* with Christ, so the world will see Him and not us. It is so hard for us to grasp this concept that we are one with Christ—I in Him and He in me. Yes, we won't complete the journey until we see Him face to face, but there is beauty in the marvelous transformation of self that we can see right here in the now.

That is why we *can* experience beauty in pain—the kind of pain which comes with transformation. When we set our eyes on the beauty of the goal, "Christ in you, the hope of glory,"[11] the

---

[11] Colossians 1:27

path becomes brighter. A vision the Lord gave me during this difficult season reflects this truth so well:

I was standing in my living room with hands raised, worshipping my Lord, praying and seeking God's face. It is one of my favorite things to do. I was caught up in the presence of God when suddenly the weight of the Holy Spirit came on me and I could no longer stand. Humbled, I found myself prostrated on the floor sobbing and weeping into the carpet. The weight of His Spirit was glorious and holy, so holy all I could do was weep. I remained there for a considerable span of time, unable to move under the weight of His love.

As I waited, a cross appeared before me. It was His cross. I was lying at the foot of Jesus' cross and when I looked up, there He was, my Jesus hanging on this massive wooden cross. I was moved by the Spirit to begin repenting of my sins, known and unknown. When I finally picked up my head, He looked down and said, "Daughter you are forgiven of your sins." Again, I was overwhelmed by the presence of His Spirit and the magnitude of His love. I began to weep again.

Jesus began to speak to me about the plans He had for my life. He asked if I was willing to trust the path He was setting before me. And, He asked if I was willing to suffer for Him? Jesus did say that it was totally up to me and He would be OK with either decision I would make. I didn't know exactly what He meant when He asked about suffering for Him. He wasn't revealing anything else, but I *knew* as I continued wait before Him that I wanted *His* plan and everything that came with His plan for me. I said, "Yes, Lord."

I have to tell you that I labored over that prophecy for many years. How exactly was I to suffer? Did this refer to my physical suffering or maybe I was to be martyred one day? No, God showed me exactly what He meant. He was asking if I was willing to suffer the pain that would be produced when He peeled back the hardened layers of my heart to heal the hurt inside. He was basically asking if I was willing for Him to take me further into His purifying process, so that I could be used in the fashion that He designed.

As I reflect now on that day, I am so glad I said, "Yes." I am able to see the beauty that was fashioned in the midst of my pain and I am overjoyed. The thing that gives me the most joy is that I am able to serve the Lord in ways that I am not sure would have been possible if I had said, "No."

I am also aware, however, of God's grace and the many opportunities He gives us to say, "Yes." My *yes* was important that day, but so were the many yeses I said along the way.

> *When you bow down before the Lord and admit your dependence on him, he will lift you up and give you honor. (James 4:10 NLT)*

Section II

Increasing Our Hunger

I realize I have said this before and I will probably say it again, *Our hunger for the Lord is probably the most important determinate for experiencing Him more fully.* Do you desire to witness the supernatural? Seek to spend more time with Jesus.

I believe I was *primed* for miracles, not that I earned them, by always taking my spiritual relationship with Jesus to the next level. There is a hunger inside of me to attain all that God has for me and wants to do through me. That hunger comes from the Holy Spirit, but I had to learn to cooperate with Him and go deeper. This is the scripture I adopted as my life scripture and I think you will see why:

> *And I pray that Christ will be more and more at home in your hearts as you trust in him. May your roots go down deep into the soil of*

> *God's marvelous love. And may you have the powers to understand, as all God's people should, how wide, how long, how high, and how deep his love really is. May you experience the love of Christ, though it is so great you will never fully understand it. Then you will be filled with the fullness of life and power that comes from God. (Ephesians 3:17–19 NLT)*

There are so many things that I could say about this passage of scripture. It stirs my heart every time I read it! I love the line, "May you experience the love of Christ, though it is so great you will never fully understand it." First of all, notice that it says, "experience the love of God." That is what I have been saying throughout these pages! We are to *experience* the love of God. To know His love we must *experience* it.

The part that blows my mind, though, is that even when we experience it, that is not the end of His love. There is always more and more and more. If we are obedient to this directive from God and allow our roots to go down deeper into His love, we will taste more of the depth, width, length and height of it.

Now, let me turn your attention to the last sentence of the Ephesians' scripture: "Then you will be filled with the fullness of life and power that comes from God." When will you be filled? "Then," after you dig deep into the love of Christ. After you have experienced His love to such a degree that it blows your mind. When you can't understand or think of such an awesome possibility! *Then* you will be filled with all the power you need to live the full life He has created for you!

Throughout this next section you will witness my thirst for God through prayer, through seeking others for prayer and through opening my heart to any manner of the supernatural. What you will see is the faithfulness of God to move in a myriad of ways—some supernatural and some *super*-supernatural. Some of the experiences I will share may stretch your thinking and your theology. Try and discern what the Spirit is showing you and please notice the outcome that each miraculous touch has had on me. The fruit in my life, from these experiences, is good fruit. The scripture tells us to test the fruit:

> *But when the Holy Spirit controls our lives, he will produce this kind of fruit in us: love, joy, peace, patience, kindness, goodness, faithfulness, gentleness, and self-control. (Galatians 5:22–23a NLT)*

Chapter Nine

Prayer

During my next many years of walking with the Lord, I grew significantly in my knowledge and experience of prayer. I discovered that prayer, our connection with God, can become an open door leading us into the supernatural. Prayer, in all its varied modes, carried me along on an awesome journey into the grand expansive depths of the Spirit. The Holy Spirit, the One who teaches us how to pray, is always faithful to guide us into the heart of God. The Spirit knows God's heart and knows how to pray in alignment with God's intentions. That is why it is so important to know the Spirit and commune with Him.

> *And because you are sons, God has sent forth the Spirit of His Son into your hearts, crying out, "Abba, Father!" (Galatians 4:5 NKJ)*

Prayer is a marvelous joining together of our spirit with the Holy Spirit of God. He will lead us into prayers that can be challenging, fulfilling, exciting, miraculous, humbling, tender, gracious, worshipful, joyful or silent. Prayer can have many words or no words. It can be sung, shouted or whispered. But, it must always be a link between the Divine and the beloved, between heaven's heart and ours.

This connection, without a doubt, is supernatural. It is us, in our earthiness, bound by space and time, touching God who is beyond space and time. And God, in His otherworldliness, reaches in to touch us in this humble place. Prayer is a uniting force which ties us to the supernatural. I believe that one of the ways my hunger for God was revived again and again was through spending those very important secret moments with Jesus.

As my hunger in the Lord continued to grow, I would literally pray for hours. I was blessed to have the time to pray, but greater than the physical reason, "I couldn't *stop* seeking Him." The Spirit continued to pull me along in this wonderful union with my God as my heart was becoming more increasingly fine-tuned to the Spirit. I was able to hear Him more deeply. At times it felt like I was more in heaven than on earth as prayer moved me deeper in my connection with God.

You may not have hours, like I did, to spend in prayer, but I want to encourage you to make time for Jesus. Ask Him to awaken your heart and make room for Him to speak to you. The more that you attune your spirit to the Holy Spirit, the greater will be your ability to notice the supernatural. One thing I have learned, as I have walked with the Lord for the past four decades, is that He loves to interact with His people.

When He interacts with us it is always with the intent of sharing His goodness and His glory with us. We are meant to spend eternity with our Lord. To do this, we must *know* Him and we must be *like* Him. This happens through our communion with our Lord and opening our lives to His supernatural ways.

It is not enough to just have a cognitive knowledge *of* God. I am deeply convinced that Jesus wants us to *experience* Him. One of the best ways to do that is through prayer. When Jesus came to this earth, His followers could physically hear Him and touch Him, but when He left, He released His Holy Spirit so that we could intimately know Him. Our God is a God who is alive. He is not dead and He wants to *live* with us and through us. This is Jesus speaking:

> *And I will pray the Father, and He will give you another Helper, that He may abide with you forever—the Spirit of truth, whom the world cannot receive, because it neither sees Him nor knows Him; but you know Him, for He dwells with you and will be in you. (John 14:16–17 NKJ)*

We step into eternity the moment we receive Jesus Christ. Jesus has not only saved us from hell and the grave, but He has lifted us up into heavenly places to be with Him right now—instantaneously. That means that we start reaping the rewards now and not just on the other side. Some of the experiences we have with God, like miracles, are solely God initiated. But, what I propose to you, is that we can *press into miracles by pressing into God.* There is work that we need to do as our part of walking with the Lord and stepping into the supernatural.

One of the ways I have learned how to move more deeply into the love of God is through contemplative or meditative type prayer. I think this kind of prayer is underplayed in the church at large and I wish there was more teaching on the practice.

I went through a period of time when I couldn't read enough on the subject. Thomas Keating's (an Episcopal Priest) books on Centering Prayer were especially helpful. I would recommend anything written by him, but a good place to start is his book *Invitation to Love.* Keating describes Christian contemplation beautifully:

> *One way God deals with the limited ways we have of relating to him is by reducing our concepts of him to silence. As resting in God in contemplative prayer becomes habitual, we spontaneously disidentify with our emotional programs for happiness and our cultural conditioning. Already we are meeting God at a deeper level. In time we will grow from a reflective relationship with God to one of communion. The latter is a being-to-being, presence to presence relationship, which is the knowledge of God in pure faith. (p. 87)*

The goal in meditative prayer is to create a space where you can focus your mind on just one thought and find that resting place in the Lord. How many times does our prayer turn into grocery lists, us instructing God on how we want Him to do thus and so? Or maybe, we start out focusing on God, but our minds take over and we start rehearsing our daily chores. There is so much in our individual worlds to distract us—the business of our schedules and demands of family, to name just two.

When the Lord directed me to start a meditation routine, I didn't know how I would do it. The time I felt I was to set was an hour in the AM and an hour in the PM. Well, looking at that schedule, TV and social demands were going to take a big dent in my commitment. However, I was sure that the directive was from God and I was desperate to find that quiet place in Him.

I warn you. At first, your exercise will feel like anything *but* prayer. The first 45–50 minutes of my meditation felt like nothing more than a mind chasing game. I would try and center on the Lord and my mind would go off in another direction. I would calmly bring it back and two-seconds later it was off again. That is the main reason people often quit this endeavor. It is hard work at first and it will feel like *rest* is no where to be found.

I would encourage you to keep trying, because it does work. The mind eventually learns how to not chatter and finally settles into that secret quiet place in the Lord. This is the place that the Lord can pour in His love unhindered by our agendas. I have found it to be a sweet place and a sacred place.

This form of prayer has also been successful in bringing much fruit into my life. I needed to learn how to quiet not only my mind, but my body and nervous system. I was a highly anxious individual and quite driven. (You could probably notice that through my previous testimony.) Additionally, there is the matter of my fierce independence.

God had a plan, though, to transform those characteristics through contemplative prayer. My posture was to lie flat on the floor and to the best of my ability yield my body, soul and spirit to the Lord. With the Holy Spirit's help, my heart's intention was pulled back again and again to the place of yielding my own agendas to Him and finding that place of surrender. It is a place where we learn *presence*—the ability to be in the moment and do nothing else except be present with the Lord.

This was not one of those supernatural transformations that was instantaneous, however. It took about a year to notice the depth of peace and surrender coming to my soul that I desired. And, it has definitely changed the way I see my Lord. I am more assured in my heart knowledge that He has everything in His control. I don't have to do summersaults in prayer getting Him to notice me or my need. He is right here with me all the time.

Furthermore, it has shifted some of my independent characteristics. The practice of putting all our attention on to the Lord and meditating on *who* He is, causes us to see Him in His bigness. I run ahead of Him less and wait more because I understand, deep in my spirit and soul, that *He* is God and He is able.

> *Be still, and know that I am God. (Psalm 46:10 NIV)*

CHAPTER TEN

MYSTICAL VISION

This next vision God graced me with, is a lovely pictoral example of what this simple unity in Christ can bring to us. I would label this vision as a mystical experience. A definition of *mystical* by Merriam-Webster is as follows: "Having a spiritual meaning that is difficult to see or understand, resulting from prayer or deep thought."[12] It is a different experience because I seemed to be caught up into a different dimension where time and place were not able to be explained through indicators we use here on earth.

What I want you to recognize is that you may not be able to understand it with your mind. It goes against some of the fundamental laws we use on earth to explain time and space. I am asking the Holy Spirit to relate to you what He wants you to receive from my experience.

This vision came at a time when I had been quieting myself before God and asking for whatever He wanted to do by His Spirit. There was a wonderful still presence of the Lord around me as I waited on God. I love that peaceful place that seems

---

[12] An Encyclopedia Brittanica Company

to quiet all my anxieties and frustrations and makes room for the supernatural. The Holy Spirit is always so faithful to meet me there. This experience, however, was way beyond what I was anticipating.

As the Holy Spirit came to me, I was lifted up and started traveling through the universes. I can't tell you if I was out of my body and actually traveling through space or if the experience was visionary in nature. I can tell you, however, that I could feel everything that was happening to me. I had sensations in my body as well as my emotions.

As I traveled, I recognized that I was in a place beyond time and matter. It was as if I could see from one universe into the next, into the next, into the next. I could sense the presence of God, but He was not separate from me. I was caught up into this universe of complete love and peace and what was so amazing to me—I was a part of it.

To say, "It was so beautiful," is so inadequate. It was beautiful in sight as well as my felt experience of it. Nothing else mattered to me—I was captivated by this pure love fusing with my soul. I did not want to be anywhere else! I was fully aware and fully present in that moment. My attention did not waver. I was 100% right there.

The Spirit first showed me the Virgin Mary while pregnant with Jesus. I heard her say, "Watch, I am going to teach you something." Instantly, I felt at one with Mary. I could feel Jesus in my womb, also—what an amazing miraculous feeling! I had a deep intuitive knowledge that even as she had to wait for the fullness of time to give birth, I had to wait for God's timing to give birth to the things He had for me. That is what Mary wanted me to learn. To *wait* suddenly felt more than OK. It felt uniquely sacred.

As I moved into sensing Mary's feelings, I was also in touch with her need for hiddenness. Here was this wonderful awesome miracle happening right inside her body and yet it had to be hidden from the world. I thought, "Would I be OK with containing the miraculous things God was doing in me until His time to reveal them?" What important lessons those are to learn. Now, I had an experience in my body that would remind me of those lessons.

After I sat awhile and took that knowledge in, the Holy Spirit led me to the next place. I looked up and saw a brilliant star-lit sky. However, there was one star that was particularly bright. I knew that it was the star marking the place of Jesus' birth. This is where time or our conception of time (linear time) again shifted. It felt as if I was right there at the birth of Jesus. I was at one with Mary and I could *feel* the angels and creation celebrating this wondrous happening. I was so filled with this eye-opening amazing joy.

Then I was walking with Jesus through the miraculous events in His life. Nevertheless, my experience wasn't linear. I wasn't experiencing one event, then the next event, etc. Each event felt as though it was happening right then. Furthermore, I experienced each event from the perspective of the one being healed.

It was an awesome experience. I *became* the leper who was healed. I *became* the man with a short limb and experienced what it felt like to have that limb grow out instantaneously. I *became* the young child who was raised from the dead. I could feel in my body as well as my emotions what they each felt when they encountered the miracle. And, it wasn't just that I was uniting with *their* feelings—it was happening right then to me.

I was feeling the awe and wonder of being healed. *I* was feeling the deep gratitude of being touched by the Almighty. *I* was feeling the amazing pleasure of actually being with Jesus.

I heard God say, "I AM the God who heals. I AM the God who heals you." I recognized that all the healing events were layered one on top of the other—as if you could view them all simultaneously. There was no separation between creation, the

Expect the Miraculous

birth of Christ and me in the here and now. I was filled with a wonderful sense of oneness and completion. The God who heals then, heals now.

Somewhere in my encounter the sensations in my body increased. My heart began to feel extremely warm. Then, I saw a light darting through the universe. It was multi-color and very vibrant. I watched as God shot it into my heart. It exploded after entering, the burning sensation increased, and my body began to vibrate.

I believe God was transforming my heart. Prior to this, I had become aware of the selfishness in my heart and my narrow, materialistic and self-centered desires. I had been in prayer, petitioning Him to change the unwanted desires. I believe this was an answer to that prayer.

Transformation was Christ's work on the cross. In His death He made it possible for our hearts to be transformed into *His* likeness. Yet again, I felt at one with the event. I could feel the deep anguish of Christ on the cross, although quickly, the Spirit moved me into His resurrection.

The light flooded me and everything around me. It was brilliant white to the site and it felt *alive* in every sense of the word. I became aware that the light was imparting something to me: wisdom. The wisdom that was being downloaded to my mind, just then, was more than I could accomplish on my own in a life-time. I knew, however, that it would take time to unfold and become clear as I lived my life. I thanked the Lord for this inspiration.

I was suddenly so grateful. Joy was exploding in my heart. The Lord asked me, "Do you want to create?" I said, "Yes, yes!" He said, "OK, make some stars." And, amazingly, I was able to do that.

I just threw them up there into the heavens. He said, "Good, good." I felt so much joy! I felt so connected to God and to every part of myself. I was aware that I was young and old at the same time. My child self was having so much fun creating.

Towards the end of this experience, I said, "Oh God, I don't want this to end." The love and the peace that surrounded me was so great. I lingered a little while longer—just soaking that great love into my heart. I asked Him, "How will I remember this?"

I felt like it was my child self asking Him that. Then, I saw Him take her hand and He grabbed a star (out of the heavens) and pressed it into her hand. I remembered that, earlier, when He showed me the stars He created, He said, "That one is you. It is Carol."

In that moment, I was mindful of my whole experience and I realized why the Lord chose a star for me to remember it. Each star was important and so vivid in my vision—the star marking the birth of Christ, the star named Carol, the stars I created along with my Creator. My child self looked down at her hand and was delighted when she saw her star. I thought, "This I will remember."

That entire experience was a lot for me to digest. I had to meditate on it awhile to comprehend what the Lord wanted me to learn from it. There are several things that were illuminated. First of all, and this one is quite obvious, is the realization that our God is a *big* God. He is so big that who He is and what He can do is sometimes way beyond our understanding.

Now, I realize that can be frustrating to us, in our humanity, because we like to figure things out—and that can include God. But, I find, when I do that, it puts God in a box and God is too big for a box. This mystical encounter reinforced that fact for me. I am not going to understand everything about God and that's OK. In fact, that is what makes God, God.

The other thing that I have noticed since my experience is that I have more contentment in the present. I have always had this anxious relationship with time—like there wasn't enough or

I would run out of it. This created in me a sense of pressure or drive to complete what I was called to do. Yes, we are to complete our calling, but not in a way that is driven by the flesh.

What this experience taught me is that from God's perspective it is already done. I am already complete. Today, I seem to relax into the present with greater ease. What was translated to me, through my experience, was this over-arching feeling that if I died right then it would be OK.

I don't know how to explain it exactly, but there was a sense of completion inside of every event, every moment—like there was nothing left out of that moment that needed to be there. And, because that moment was complete, all the other moments were complete. From a linear perspective we could say that God sees the end from the beginning, but from God's perspective that really isn't accurate. In eternity, there is no beginning and no end. We are complete right now.

So, here I am, again, left with the dilemma of explaining the unexplainable—explaining how all of what you read above of my vision affected and transformed my life. And, all I can think of is one word, "Love." I realize that it sounds too simple and yet it is not. When you have tasted this kind of love, it is all you can think about when you think of God.

I know the scripture, "God is love." (I John 4:8b NKJ) But even quoting that scripture is not enough. I want to shout, "God's love is bigger—much, much bigger." It extends throughout all eternity. It is big enough to swallow up any sin. It is big enough to search us out inside any darkness, which hides us. It fills us and expands us, just like our breath. It is full of grace, mercy, fiery passion and forgiveness. It is unconditional and transforming. It is everything.

> *And I am convinced that nothing can ever separate us from his love. Death can't, and life can't. The angels can't, and the demons*

can't. Our fears for today, our worries about tomorrow, and even the powers of hell can't keep God's love away. Whether we are high above the sky or in the deepest ocean, nothing in all creation will ever be able to separate us from the love of God that is revealed in Christ Jesus our Lord. (Romans 8:38–39 NLT)

Chapter Eleven

Surprised by Joy

One thing that I would like you to understand about me—in the midst of all the glorious miracles that were happening to me, I am still flesh and blood. In the beginning of my amazing walk with God, my life was full of highs and lows. As I revealed to you, there were hurts from my past that needed to be healed, hang-ups in my behavior patterns that needed to be changed, and some mental illness, in the form of depression, that needed to be healed. There were deep valley experiences dispersed throughout my mountain top encounters.

    I am thankful, however, for each experience, positive and negative. I must admit I would much rather abide on the mountain top, but that is not God's perfect plan for me. Neither is it His plan for you. We are challenged to grow in our faith and challenged to mature in our character through every valley experience. Since I have walked with Jesus for four decades, my yoyo experiences have mellowed out a great deal, but that is only because I allowed God to do the work He wanted to do in me for all those years.

What I am very grateful for, nevertheless, was the surprise gifts of joy that Jesus had for me along the way. You will see, in the next few stories, how His heavenly joy came and exploded in my spirit—refreshing me, imparting life to me and giving me the courage to go on. The phenomena I am speaking of is usually referred to as *laughing in the Spirit*. This phenomena not only is a sign and wonder from the Lord, but I believe it is also a powerful healing agent for the spirit and soul. It is the Holy Spirit who imparts the joy of the Lord to us:

> *Now may the God of hope fill you with all joy and peace in believing, that you may abound in hope by the power of the Holy Spirit. (Romans 15:13 NKJ)*

Of course, we are to possess the *joy* of our salvation. The deep abiding joy that comes when we can grasp that our sins have been forgiven and we have been ushered into the kingdom of our Lord, Jesus Christ. However, there is also a joy that is released by the Holy Spirit to heal our hearts and lift our spirits. I've experienced this release of joy many times. Let me share one of my experiences with you.

Throughout my years of serving the Lord, I have had several prayer partners. I have found this practice to be encouraging to me because the Holy Spirit is so faithful to be present to our needs when we meet together. Whenever Tony and I could, we would also pray with other couples. A meeting for dinner would often turn into a "Holy Ghost prayer meeting." That is what happened this particular evening.

Pete and Patty, our dear friends and prayer partners, invited Tony and I to dinner. Patty and I had become intercessory warriors together and Pete was very instrumental in discipling Tony throughout his early Christian experience. And, we had come to a place of really valuing their friendship.

We arrived at their door on time and Pete greeted us with his always relaxed demeanor and wide smile that made one feel so comfortable in their lovely home. What I noticed right away, is what I usually noticed—a distinct presence of the Holy Spirit. Since both Pete and Patty were prayer warriors, the felt presence of the Spirit often remained after meetings and meditations.

Pete graciously took my coat and I settled into their sofa, relaxing into that marvelous spiritual ambience. Patty peeked around the corner of the dining area to say, "Hi" as she busied herself with the finishing details of the dinner table. I couldn't help noticing that the table was dressed to the max with a gorgeous arrangement of fresh garden flowers adorning the center, which sent an amazing fragrance flittering throughout the room. I asked Patty if she wanted my help, but she declined my offer. Both Pete and Patty have a gift for making one feel comfortable and loved in their home. That is exactly how I felt.

Dinner was delicious, as always. Patty is a great cook. And, the conversation was very up-lifting. Since we had spiritual connections with one another, our conversation usually circled back to the Lord, which caused me to feel spiritually as well as physically fed. Both were very good.

After we were through eating, of course, we all agreed that we needed to pray for each other. Patty asked, "How have you been feeling lately, Carol?" They both were very much aware of the physical pain I had been suffering from and the depression that went with it. Because of our trusting relationship, I didn't mind being honest regarding the depth of depression that I had been experiencing. Do you know that when we can be open and transparent with one another that creates an atmosphere where the Holy Spirit is free to move? And He *did* decide to move!

Pete asked if he could pray for me and I answered, "Of course." Pete put his hand on my head and prayed very simply, "Holy Spirit, would you fill my sister, Carol, with joy." Well, I don't think he expected what happened next (nor did I.) In an instant, I was filled with so much joy that I burst out in profound laughter. I know that I had never laughed like that in my lifetime. It was a deep gut laughter that flooded my whole body. Pete took his hand away quickly and looked half startled and half amazed. Everyone just stared at me and I couldn't stop laughing.

The joy that I was feeling in my heart and spirit was so huge I couldn't contain it. I sat there and laughed and praised Jesus for over an hour. They joined me in praising God, though all of us were a little overwhelmed. None of us had ever experienced anything like this before. This was my first time, and thankfully it was not my last laughing release.

I can't fully put into words what transpired in my heart in this process. But, what I can say is that it was awesome and grand—like something was breaking open on the inside that was dead. I felt more alive, more present in my body. There were tears with the laughter, however they were good tears. The Holy Ghost joy was bursting forth on the inside and the gush of the Spirit was pushing all the despair out.

I realized quickly, after this experience, that Jesus wanted to bring me joy. Even in the midst of my depression and whatever was causing it, Jesus Christ had joy for me. It was around this time that I began visiting a church in Toronto, Canada called (at the time) the Toronto Airport Fellowship. What drove me to that church was a book I happened to pick up (a God directed coincidence) one day in the Christian bookstore called *Catch the Fire* by Guy Chevreau. I found it so exhilarating I couldn't put it down.

It included many miraculous testimonies from a revival that was breaking out in their church. At this point in my Christian walk, I had never heard of revivals. Although my husband and I were saved in the revival that swept through the US in the 1970s, we weren't aware of this powerful movement as a force of change. The Toronto Blessing Revival (which the Toronto revival then became labeled) began in Toronto, Canada and swept through Florida (USA), England and other parts of Europe.

I was so excited by the testimonies in the book and so hungry for more of God that I decided to take the trip up to Toronto. God had given me a taste of His marvelous joy and it stirred my heart to ask my Jesus for more. I convinced a female friend of mine from church, Janice, to go with me. We quickly purchased tickets and were on our way to a new adventure.

When we arrived at the Toronto church, a converted warehouse big enough to hold the large number of people traveling there, I noticed that I had never seen nor experienced the manifestations present. Individuals were shaking under the power of God, jumping up and down, laughing, falling off their chairs and rolling on the floor. I didn't know whether to scream, "Eek!" and run away, or to enjoy that part of me that was simply intrigued. Since I have an adventurous nature when it comes to the things of God, I sighed an internal, "Wow!" and I quickly determined that I would watch, wait and pray.

You have probably noticed thus far that the Lord seems to give me the experience first and then the explanation for the experience. It is just how He works with me. It might have something to do with the way I learn and process. I am a jump in first and process later kind-of person.

If you are someone who has to cognitively process something before tasting the experience, there is nothing inherently wrong with this approach. However, if you stay in your head and your cognitive reasoning and avoid your emotions, you may miss the depth of the experience. After all, that is what I have been emphasizing in this writing—the *experiencing* part of knowing the Lord.

The thing that I quickly noticed, when I looked around at the various people who made up the congregation, was how much these people loved Jesus. Their worship simply amazed me. It was filled with animation: jumping up and down, smiling, laughing, dancing, waving arms and banners, and shouting. Furthermore, the worship didn't stop. After one hour, the band was still playing and the people were still worshipping. The pastors didn't seem concerned that they were not preaching yet. They, in fact, were lined up in the front row jumping, clapping and shouting with everyone else.

Then laughter broke out quite loudly from the back of the gathering. It was really hard to ignore what seemed like chaos coming from this whole group of people. I was more than interested to see what the pastor would do in this situation. Pastor Arnott finally went up to the platform, but he just stood there for a good amount of time praising God.

Then, in the midst of the laughter and noise, he invited all of those people to come down front to the altar. I couldn't believe my eyes. I never saw anything like it, especially in church. The people looked drunk. Some of them could not stand and they were being supported by others. Some of the people were still laughing and others were crying. It took them awhile to get down front because occasionally one or two would fall on the floor and be unable to walk any further.

When they arrived at the altar, Pastor Arnott began asking them what God was doing. They told him that during the worship the Holy Spirit began touching their hearts. There were a number of them that were saved on the spot and fell down weeping. Others were experiencing deliverance over some bondage in their lives. Still others were filled with exuberant joy and couldn't stop praising Jesus. Some were filled with the Spirit and began speaking in tongues.

My excitement peaked. I had never seen an instantaneous corporate move of God before. God was indeed touching these people. My heart was filled with gratitude to the Lord for the amazing way He was moving in lives. Their testimonies gave evidence of the fruit of the Holy Spirit. At times, laughter broke out throughout the congregation and I joined in for another dose of joy from the Lord.

This was just the beginning of the outpouring I witnessed and experienced over a decade of visiting the Toronto revival. Yes, I went back every year for ten years. It was the love of God revealed to me through every miraculous encounter which drew me back for more. Furthermore, the fruit in my life that I gained was, without a doubt, from the workings of the Holy Spirit that I experienced at those times.

> *You will know them by their fruits... Even so, every good tree bears good fruit, but a bad tree bears bad fruit. A good tree cannot bear bad fruit, nor can a bad tree bear good fruit... Therefore by their fruits you will know them. (Matthew 7: 16–18, 20 NKJ)*

Chapter Twelve

Depression Healed

Depression was something that followed me throughout much of my adult life. The miraculous encounters I experienced with God did mitigate the symptoms quite a bit. However, there came a time when I realized it had lingered far too long. That motivated me to start seeing a therapist to aid with the issues I carried forward from childhood. I also saw a doctor for my condition and started taking anti-depressant medications.

Jesus Christ is indeed a supernatural God. And yet, Jesus heals in many different ways. Often, the supernatural and the natural overlap because, it is my deep belief, that God is *always* interacting with our lives. I had been praying for some time for Jesus to heal the depression, but I didn't want to miss the more natural way that He may be wanting to heal me. It may be harder for us to recognize *the natural* as an act of God, but if we look closely, we will see the hand of God in our everyday lives.

I am a very thorough person, so I covered all my bases. Along with a therapist, medication, and prayer, I decided to go to the Toronto church for some healing prayer. It was my first night there and I already was so blessed with the worship and preaching. It was quite late at night, but no one seemed to pay attention to time up there. The men started stacking the chairs, which was the cue that prayer for individuals would start soon.

I was so caught up in the feel good of the service that I almost forgot what I wanted prayer for. I silenced my mind and asked the Lord to show me what He wanted to do. He said, "I want to heal you from depression." I had been praying for that healing for so long, so I said to the Lord, "I believe; help my unbelief."

The band started playing some soft worship music and I moved in front of the next prayer person that was available. I told her what I needed prayer for and she was very encouraging. She shared with me, "I received prayer for the very same thing last year and God healed me. I have had no depression since." Needless to say, that lifted my faith some more. I was open to whatever Jesus wanted to do.

She prayed a very simple prayer and my body fell over in the Spirit. The pastors instruct everyone to lie on the floor as long as you want to take in from the Holy Spirit, so I did just that. As I lay there, I began to feel more and more joy flood into my spirit and soul. The pastor started speaking to us, "I sense another wave of the Holy Spirit coming." Every time he spoke that declaration, I could actually feel waves of the Holy Spirit flowing through me. I wanted to stay there forever. In actuality, I was there about an hour. After I got up, and thereafter, I was freed from that debilitating depression.

Jesus Christ is in the business of healing us body and soul, emotions and mind, and of course, spirit. Sometimes when we have been healed in a certain area, it is that very area where we can pray for someone else and see them healed. (You saw that in my example of the woman who prayed for me.) Also, our gifting may also coincide with our occupation. I, more often, witness *soul* healing happening through me. That lines up with my natural gifting and my career as a psychotherapist.

Jesus is not limited, though, in the ways He chooses to heal us or heal through us. I have found that the more we can stay *open* and *alert* to His leading and directives, the more that Jesus is free to complete *His* desires. Here is a scripture that talks about having readiness for Christ's return. It is speaking about the Lord's second coming; however, I believe it is applicable for whenever the Lord draws near to us. We can ask ourselves the question, "Will I be ready?" Or, maybe a better question is, "Am I ready now?"

> *Be dressed for service and well prepared, as though you were waiting for your master to return from the wedding feast. Then you will be ready to open the door and let him in the moment he arrives and knocks. There will be special favor for those who are ready and waiting for his return. I tell you, he himself will seat them, put on an apron, and serve them as they sit and eat! (Luke 12:35–37 NLT)*

Jesus may show up in the manner that we do not expect Him. Are we going to stay alert enough that we can recognize Him and open the door and let Him in? There are so many various ways that the Lord has shown Himself to me and visited me. I am so glad that I opened the door.

That doesn't mean that we ignore asking critical questions concerning our experience. Nevertheless, sometimes over-analysis is our attempt to avoid the vulnerability that our encounter with God would require. A question that is usually helpful is this: "Is this something that the love of God would impart?"

We can also examine the results of the God experience with the question: "Is this result evidence of the working of the Spirit?" No matter how strange the experience may appear, the aftereffects should exhibit good fruit. For me, one of the strangest examples in the Word of God concerning a healing by Jesus was the healing of the blind man at Bethsaida.

> *When they arrived at Bethsaida, some people brought a blind man to Jesus, and they begged him to touch and heal the man. Jesus took the blind man by the hand and led him out of the village. Then, spitting on the man's eyes, he laid his hands on him and asked, "Can you see anything now?"*
>
> *The man looked around. "Yes," he said, "I see people, but I can't see them very clearly. They look like trees walking around."*
>
> *Then Jesus placed his hands over the man's eyes again. As the man stared intently, his sight was completely restored, and he could see everything clearly. (Mark 8:22–25 NLT)*

I wonder what we would think today if we saw a minister spit on someone's eyes? Would we be quick to dismiss the miracle? Maybe God included the details of this miracle in His Word, so that we would not be quick to discount our encounters with Him. If we get caught up with examining the propriety of the action, we might miss the miracle.

The ways we think about God are formed through our upbringing, culture and education, including spiritual education. Those influences can cause us to put God in a box when what we need to do is gain a vision of God *outside of the box*. God is a big God who can and will act in ways outside of our thinking.

Yes, the Word of God does present the Lord accurately where it comes to miracles, but for the most part, people have stopped anticipating the miraculous move of God in their lives.

Even the Christian community differs on their beliefs concerning present-day miracles. Why is this?

I think one of the main reasons is that we human beings like to understand things. There is a great emphasis, in this present age, on increasing our knowledge. The pursuit of knowledge has taken front stage over any other human endeavor. This also correlates with the human need to gain control of one's life. Together, these pursuits tend to push the pursuit of God and God's ways to the side. Even when seeking a Christian way of life, one can easily end up molding God into our own image (box), instead of being changed into His image. Fr. Paul Coutinho, author of, *How Big is Your God?* explains:

> *In a similar fashion, the Christian mystics tell us—and I've come to understand through personal experience—that if we want to get deeper into the river of divine life, if we want to know an infinitely big God, then we too will have to transcend the images of God that we might have. The Divine is so great, so wondrous, so unfathomable that any image or metaphor we hang on God is at best only a partial fit and quickly limits our ability to experience other aspects. (p. 48)*

Each time I experience a miracle, my thought processes are stretched. My view of *who God is* has to expand. However, to embrace the miracle as a miracle, as something that comes to me from a supernatural God, I have to embrace it with my spiritual/intuitive being. I cannot attach to the miracle solely through my understanding because my understanding will minimize the miracle. Our intellect cannot comprehend the marvelous workings of God. We can only but yield to the mystery that is contained in God, the reality that He is a big God and our thinking is really very small.

> *"My thoughts are completely different from yours," says the Lord. "And my ways are far beyond anything you would imagine. For just as the heavens are higher than the earth, so are my ways higher than your ways and my thoughts higher than your thoughts." (Isaiah 55:8–9 NLT)*

Chapter Thirteen

Mountainside Experience

I have a dear friend and prayer partner named Christy. I guess the best word I have to describe her is *faithful*. She has stood with me through some of my darkest times and together we have experienced some of the most joyous miraculous interventions of God. One of the things we especially enjoy is traveling together to spiritual conferences and retreats. The deep love and fervency for Jesus that we share has knit our hearts together.

One retreat we attended together was exceptionally momentous. It was at The Center for Prayer Mobilization (CPM) in Idyllwild, CA. We both had high expectations of what God would do and so we chatted excitedly on our travel up the mountain. When Christy and I get together it is so easy for us to fill our conversation with talk of the Lord. Our prayer experiences together were many and spiritually, we speak the same language. We have the kind of relationship where one of us can begin a sentence and the other one can finish it.

There is such a deep sense of peace that comes over me when I travel to a mountain place to pray. Each turn of the road brings into sight another view of God's majestic beauty. I love the quiet and the serenity of it. Traffic noises are no more. Instead, the wind and birds weave a harmonic melody so pleasant to the soul.

The brisk air tells me that my altitude is climbing. As it sifts through my window and brushes against my skin, I feel invigorated. My thoughts seem to swell with excitement and anticipation, "My God, here I am—waiting to meet with you inside my mountain sanctuary." We had a difficult time finding the turnoff and had to turn around and go back a bit, but that did not silence my impassioned soul.

I pulled into the dirt parking area, which was situated in the center of the cabins. We were instructed to go the dining hall to get our keys and directions to the cabin we were to stay in. Christy and I were disappointed that we were not assigned to the same cabin. But, even that disappointment couldn't quench the heightened anticipation that I felt.

The cabins were rustic, but very cute. The heaters were not all together efficient, so I didn't waste any time finding the sweats I had packed. We would enjoy a dinner together in the dining hall before our first evening meeting. I grabbed my flashlight and another layer of clothing and headed towards the dining hall. When I entered, I was so glad to find that room warm and toasty. Christy had gotten there first and saved a place for me at her table.

Everyone was friendly and seemed to be sharing our excitement. We sang a few choruses before dinner and I could feel the presence of the Spirit. It reminded me of some of the other uplifting camp experiences I've had. It always feels wonderful to leave all my cares behind me and make room for the Lord.

The weekend fulfilled all my expectations. Worship was wonderful. One of the nights we worshipped for about four hours, and heaven drew very near. Their prophetic team gave us all words of direction and encouragement. My word from God had to do with the healing ministry which would flow through me. That was another confirmation from God that I was going in the right direction.

After the last morning meeting, we had to say our good-byes, which was always bittersweet to me. It is always difficult saying good-bye to such a high spiritual time and it was especially hard to say good-bye to these women I had gotten to know so intimately within the last three days. That is the sweet thing about the Holy Spirit. He takes strangers and draws them together with the Lord in a beautiful bond that goes beyond the natural.

Christy had already gotten into the car. I stood outside and looked around, one last time, at the mighty trees surrounding this holy place. My soul longed to drink in the last bit of what God had for me in that place. I waited. Finally, I opened the car door and slid behind the steering wheel. It was time to go.

As we started our travels down this lovely mountainside both Christy and I were silent, the kind of silence that grows out of satisfaction. I was rehearsing in my mind some of the wonderful ways God had met me. I felt so full and so thankful.

After several minutes Christy said, "Carol, did you bring any flowers in the car?" I said, "No, why?" She said, "I smell flowers. Maybe it is the countryside." I was smelling it, too, and opened my window to see if it was outside. Nevertheless, it was not.

By this time the scent was getting stronger. I don't know which one of us said it first, "Maybe it's the Lord!" When that phrase was spoken, the flowery scent increased even more. What an awesome experience! It felt as though we were being bathed in the scent of the Lord. The excitement in my spirit was building and building until I just had to sing praises to God. Christy said she was feeling the same way and we both began singing one chorus after another.

We began to notice that, every time we sang a chorus, a fresh wave of His scent filled the car. It seemed like the Lord was letting us know how much He enjoyed it, encouraging us to keep singing. We never stopped singing as we traveled down the mountain and His wonderful presence continued with us. We started giggling out of the sheer enjoyment of the experience.

Then, we began to notice that the Lord seemed to like one chorus over the others. Every time we sang the chorus, "I love you, Lord and I lift my voice, to worship You, oh my Lord rejoice!" the scent became heavier and heavier. It was so delightful to be able to experience the delight of the Lord as we worshipped Him. His enjoyment increased our enjoyment. The more He poured His love upon us, the more love we had to give Him. That is exactly what our love relationship with the Lord is meant to look like.

> *Your love is more delightful than wine. Pleasing is the fragrance of your perfumes; your name is like perfume poured out... Take me away with you—let us hurry! (Song of Songs 1:2b–4a NIV)*

The Lord's fragrance continued with us for our two hour drive home. We became immersed in this lovely composition of song, laughter, tears and waves of heavenly perfume. We both began to share the visions the Lord was giving us. We saw similar visions of Christ's dining with us. He set the table in beautiful china, golden utensils and candles. He pulled out the chairs for us to be seated and served the meal to us before He sat to dine with us. He then shared with us His words of love and adoration. They poured like sweetness from His lips and were bathed in the scent of His presence.

I don't know how I was driving; I was so overcome by the Spirit. We truly were dining with our Lord that day. I echo the sweet words of Solomon:

> *"Take me away with you—let us hurry!"*
> (Song of Songs 1:4a NIV)

Chapter Fourteen

Raised from the Dead

When examining the different types of miracles that Jesus performs, I am especially intrigued over the resurrection of the dead. I do believe it is because the resurrection is so internally wired to who I am as a spiritual being. The resurrection is the corner stone of our faith. If Christ was not risen from the dead, there would be no faith—at least no *living* faith.

When we think of the scriptures that speak of the dead raising to life, certainly, one of the most prominent ones (outside of our Lord, of course) is Lazarus. We know, because of the account in John,[13] that Lazarus was dead for four days.[14] We are also told,

> *Now Jesus loved Martha and her sister and Lazarus. (John 11:5 NIV)*

---

[13] John 11
[14] John 11: 39

So, if Jesus loved Lazarus, why did He wait four days to go to him when He heard that Lazarus was sick? Jesus had a plan.

Jesus wanted His followers to think about resurrection in a new way. Passover was coming and the season when Christ, himself, would be persecuted and die. How would His disciples be able to grasp what He was about to tell them of His own death and resurrection? In the raising of Lazarus, He was giving them a powerful picture of not only His resurrection, but also their future resurrection.

> *Now Martha said to Jesus, "Lord, if You had been here, my brother would not have died..." Jesus said to her, "I am the resurrection and the life. He who believes in Me, though he may die, he shall live. And whoever lives and believes in Me shall never die. Do you believe this?" (John 11:21, 25–26 NKJ)*

Therefore, I believe that when Jesus decides to resurrect the dead, He is giving the witnesses a *sign* that is the evidence of who He is. Jesus said, "I am the resurrection and the life."[15] What better sign than raising someone from the dead!

Here is my resurrection story. My children, like so many other children, love animals. Especially when they were young, we housed all kinds of animals: mice, rats, guinea pigs, rabbits, turtles, dogs, hamsters and fish. (Praise God it wasn't all at the same time!) The kids became very attached to each one of them.

Now, there was a stretch of time when we had several fish and one of the fish died. It wasn't hard to recognize. He was floating on top of the water, his gills were not moving and he lost all of his color. The kids were sad and so, I decided to pray for him.

---

[15] John 11: 25

I had been learning about the gifts of the Spirit in church and, like I said earlier, I was intrigued with the raising of the dead. I felt like this would be good practice. Several times that day I went in and put one finger on the fish and prayed. I realize this may sound silly, but I felt a deep desire to do this. By the end of the day, he was still the same.

My kids were watching this whole process and they asked me, "Is my fish going to live?" I told them, "That is what we are praying for. Jesus can do anything." They went with me as I prayed for him one more time and we went to bed for the evening.

Well, you guessed it. The next morning I heard my children shout, "Mommy, mommy, he is alive!" Sure enough, I ran into their room and there he was swimming around the bowl. He had returned to his normal color and vigor. My children were so excited they ran to tell all their friends. Though my story may seem so little compared to other stories of the dead being raised, yet I know it wasn't little to my children. What a wonderful picture Jesus gave them of His resurrection power.

Heidi Baker, a missionary in Africa, reports that she and her team have seen many people raised from the dead. It is one of the tools the Holy Spirit uses to bring the whole community to salvation in Jesus. It is not surprising to me that God chooses that method, echoing the risen Lord proclaiming, "This is who I am. I am alive and I have the power to raise you into new life." One of the accounts from Heidi Baker's book *Always Enough,* Pastor Rego's story, moved me so much I have to share it here:

> *Recently I was with my brothers in the Lord from the church. We felt God call us to pray and fast for three days with no water or food. The second night of our fast somebody came to my house...he told me his wife died. I*

went with him… His wife's head was covered already.

Suddenly I felt something touch me. I thought, "Oh, God, I need to pray now for you to give me the power to do a miracle." I remember Peter did miracles. I'd like to be like Peter. Who said we can't do this, too? So I got up. I started to feel strength and great power coming into me.

I told everyone to be quiet and not cry anymore, because this mother who died is a Christian… We sang and worshiped the Lord… I got next to this dead mother. I took the cover off her head and began to pray. I prayed for over an hour. She was very cold. The second hour I started to feel warmth coming into her. I could feel her body warming up. I prayed all the way down her body. When I got down to her legs, the bottom of her legs were still cold.

I picked her up, and then her eyes were open. She began to vomit and vomit… I told a woman, "Sit here and hold her," because she could see everybody now. "Let's keep praying," I said. Her legs were beginning to get warm. We prayed some more. The third hour her whole body had movement. She was alive!… So we took her and carried her to church. It was Saturday, and we spent the whole night in prayer. She began to speak… Our church is full now. This is a wonderful miracle in our church that helped it to grow." (pp. 74–76)

The thing that really grips me regarding this story is that life did not come into this woman instantaneously. The pastor and church had to have enough faith and conviction to keep praying. What if they had stopped after two hours or didn't pray through the night?

I realize I didn't give up on my children's fish; although sadly, I don't know if I could have been that diligent with a human being. We can get so caught up in protecting our image and not looking foolish. Does that keep us from the miraculous?

> *But without faith it is impossible to please Him, for he who comes to God must believe that He is, and that He is a rewarder of those who diligently seek Him. (Hebrews 11:6 NKJ)*

Chapter Fifteen

Gold Teeth

The sign and wonder I am going to describe to you next, will probably stretch your thinking a bit, as it did mine. Nonetheless, it is a miracle that is worthy of our attention because of the amazing way it reveals the extravagant nature of God. This is my first hand account of the sign and wonder, impartation by God, of gold teeth.

    When you first hear of it, it can seem silly and so unlike God, but is it? I would like you to remember that signs and wonders, like other supernatural interventions, reveal something about the nature of God, how He relates to His people and what He wants us to learn from them. Jesus' first miracle on this earth was a sign and wonder. It occurred at a wedding, when He turned the water into wine. At first glance, it seems like a strange miracle for Christ to perform, especially since it was His first. Let's take a deeper look.

> *Jesus said to the servants, "Fill the jars with water;" so they filled them to the brim. Then he told them, "Now draw some out and take it to*

> *the master of the banquet." They did so, and the master of the banquet tasted the water that had been turned into wine. He did not realize where it had come from, though the servants who had drawn the water knew. (John 2:7–9 NIV)*

Notice that the miracle was not done to impress anyone. The master of the banquet and probably the guests did not recognize that a miracle had been performed. Now let's look at who the miracle was for:

> *This, the first of his miraculous signs, Jesus performed in Cana of Galilee. He thus revealed his glory, and his disciples put their faith in him. (John 2:11 NIV)*

His disciples were most likely sitting close to Him and so they were able to observe what He did. Jesus was revealing to them His deity, whereby shifting their relationship with Him—which was a vitally important shift for them if they were to follow Him as His disciples and be witnesses of His Godhead. Again, we can see that Jesus was strategic in His timing and execution of this miracle.

Eric Metaxas in his book, *Miracles*, describes another sign and wonder—the opening of the Red Sea[16] and postulates why God might have chosen that miracle for that specific time:

> *The point of this, and most other miracles, is that no one would ever forget it. So how can something have not been dramatically out of the ordinary when we see that it was meant to forever change the way the Israelites perceived*

---

[16] Exodus 14:21–31

> God and themselves? In fact, it was the ultimate mnemonic device. Whenever the Israelites would doubt God after that event, whenever they doubted that he had chosen them and made them his own people in an unprecedented way, whenever they doubted that he had a plan for them and a path for them and a future for them, they only needed to remember what he had done back there when the army of Pharaoh was bearing down upon them to annihilate them forever. They would remember that it had really happened, that God is not just real but that he is that real, so real that he sometimes intervenes in dramatic ways. (pp. 19–20)

So, my challenge to you is this: Will you carry that thought with you—*that God is not just real but that he is that real, so real that he sometimes intervenes in dramatic ways*—as you read my account of the gold teeth miracle? We will be reflecting on the questions: What does this reveal about the nature of God? Why would God relate to His people in this way? What are we to learn?

I was visiting, again, my favorite church, Toronto Airport Fellowship. I stepped off the plane totally expectant and excited about what God was going to do. Jesus never failed to meet me on my trips to Toronto, so my expectations were high. I could never predict what God would do, however, because it was always something different—but wonderful different.

This was the first time I had flown up during the winter. Coming from Los Angeles I had to scrape together some winter clothes, but I was confident that I was well prepared *until* I stepped outside of the airline terminal. Wow, I didn't remember cold air taking your breath away! I had grown up in New York, and had encountered the cold weather, but this experience seems to have slipped my memory. I tried wrapping my neck scarf around my mouth and nose, and hunted for my gloves (which were stuffed somewhere in my purse) and head across the terminal towards my hotel shuttle.

Somehow I managed to get to my room in sort of one piece. The top of my head hurt, though, because I was so cold. I hadn't remembered that experience either. I had about an hour before the first evening service, so I turned up the thermostat in my room and submerged myself beneath the bedcovers until I got warm. That was the goal.

As I lay there, peeking my head out tentatively from my down cocoon, I wondered why I thought a winter trip might be exciting. I think it was the whole nostalgia thing of maybe seeing a snow fall again (which I missed since moving to California.) Nonetheless, even that thought did not seem to excite me right then.

When my body warmed up some, and I determined that I wasn't going to die of the cold, I decided that I had better make the best of it. I glanced at the clock and realized my time was running out if I was still planning to get the shuttle to the church. I searched my suitcase for another layer of clothing, my bible and journal and ran for the shuttle. (During conferences the church ran a shuttle to all the main hotels, which was very helpful.)

I found a vacant seat in the sanctuary and introduced myself to the woman sitting next to me. She had traveled there from the UK. Because people flew in from all over the world, I was always excited to meet everyone. That was one of the things I came to enjoy in my travels to the Toronto church.

As I settled into my seat, she started telling me about the miracle of gold teeth. She was there the day before and had witnessed the occurrence. She was quite excited as she shared some of the stories with me. Later that evening I asked several other people about the gold teeth miracles and they said it had been happening up there for several months. True to my nature—I was very excited to find out more about this amazing occurrence. And, I thought, "Maybe it will happen to me!"

Now I do realize that my response may not be yours right this second, but try to keep an open mind. If you believe that Jesus turned water into wine, and you believe that He could work the same kind of miracles today, then what would be the problem with a few gold teeth? Well, it was actually more than a *few* gold teeth. I watched over the next five days, as hundreds of people received gold teeth or dental miracles.

It was really quite simple. The pastor asked the congregation to look into each other's mouths (to check if there were presently any gold teeth.) Then, he asked us to lay hands on our jaws while he prayed, "Jesus, do a miracle." We then looked into each other's mouths again to see if there were gold teeth. It was funny while we were doing it, but exciting.

There were cameras set up on the platform and everyone who knew they had received a gold tooth went up. When they opened their mouths, the camera picked up the image and flashed it on the large screen. Some people received as many as three or four gold teeth. Let me clarify something, the gold teeth were not replacing good teeth. They either replaced old silver fillings, old caps, bridges or dental work that needed to be done.

One woman testified that she had received a gold cap a month ago and went to her dentist to check it out. He took a bit of the gold and had it analyzed by a jeweler. The jeweler said the gold was very pure and he had certainly never seen anything like it before.

There were so many testimonies of how God had used this miracle to do other miracles in people's lives. One woman told her unbelieving husband that she was going to a meeting where individuals were receiving gold teeth. He scoffed at her and said, "If you get a gold tooth, I will give myself to God." She got three gold teeth, went home and showed him and he gave his life to the Lord.

Many non-Christians who were present received gold teeth and then received the Lord. There was so much excitement in the room. People were jumping out of their chairs and running around shouting. It felt like God having fun with His children. More than fun, He was also showing His people in a tangible way just how much He loves us. That is what is so wonderful about miracles of this sort—they are an evidence of His majesty (how really big He is) and an evidence of His love.

Through the whole experience, I couldn't stop thinking about the heavenly streets of gold. It was like the Lord was dropping a bit of heavenly gold into His children's mouths and uncovering His extravagance. He is an extravagant God, extravagant with His wealth and with His love. I was so blessed to have that experience, even though I didn't get a gold tooth. I had plenty of evidence around me to confirm that this was not only *a* miracle, but *many* miracles.

So, to answer my earlier questions: What does this reveal about the nature of God? My first answer I think is very obvious— He is a very big God who can act in many various ways. But, I think it also reveals that God is concerned about every aspect of our lives, big or small. If God pays attention to a tooth, which we may consider incidental, then maybe we can see the loving way He cares about every part of our lives.

The second question: Why would God relate to His people in that way? Speaking from my experience, I felt so much joy and excitement in the room. We were behaving like children on Christmas morning, opening a gift from under the tree. We are God's children, aren't we? It felt so much like God having fun, giving His children gifts and enjoying our delight at receiving them. If we enjoy giving our children gifts, how much more must God gain pleasure in blessing us?

The third question: What are we to learn? I believe we are to learn that God *is* a giver of gifts and that we should never be afraid to ask for anything, big or small. The gold teeth tell us that

He is extravagant! We can go to Him with any concern on our hearts.

Furthermore, the gold teeth were a sign to many people who then gave their lives to Him. It was a physical, tangible sign that could not be refuted. Praise God that He has so many ways to show His love for us and draw us to Himself.

> *Jesus did many other miraculous signs in the presence of his disciples, which are not recorded in this book. But these are written that you may believe that Jesus is the Christ, the Son of God, and that by believing you may have life in his name. (John 20:30–31 NIV)*

Chapter Sixteen

The Comforter

In this last decade of my life, I have experienced the passing of my dear husband, Tony. As he transitioned into his heavenly home March 3, 2013, I discovered that grief has a way of grabbing your heart and taking your breath away. His death left me feeling so empty and lost. I knew, in my mind, that these are normal reactions, but my sorrow was greater than I imagined it would be. In my distress, I cried out for God to meet me and, in His faithfulness, He answered me through another wondrous sign.

One of the names for the Holy Spirit is the Comforter and although I have felt His comfort at other times in my life, the miraculous way through which the Lord touched my current grief, moved me deeply.

Jesus knows about grief because He experienced it. The bible states that, "He wept," at the tomb of His friend, Lazarus.[17] Agonizing sorrow gripped His soul in the Garden of

---

[17] John 11:35

Gethsemane.[18] And, Jesus cried out in the midst of His darkest grief on the cross:

> And about the ninth hour Jesus cried out with a loud voice, saying, "Eli, Eli, lama sabachthani?" that is "My God, My God, why have You forsaken Me?" (Matthew 27:46 NKJ)

Our reactions to loss and grief can vary from circumstance to circumstance and person to person. Elizabeth Kubler-Ross, a Swiss psychiatrist who studied the effects of grief, outlined the five stages in her book, *On Death and Dying*. They are: denial, anger, bargaining, depression, and acceptance. They are not progressive steps, however. We can jump back and forth from one stage to another until we finally settle on acceptance. There are also no fixed time-tables for our recovery, but the Holy Spirit can shorten the process and bring us His comfort in our distress. God promises to be with us in our sorrow and He is faithful to His promise:

> I will turn their mourning into joy. I will comfort them and exchange their sorrow for rejoicing. (Jeremiah 31:13b NLT)

Tony's illnesses were multiple, and he was ill for a total of five years. He had emphysema, congestive heart failure and prostate cancer that eventually metastasized into the bone. At the beginning of his illness he was hospitalized for three months. He had contracted various infections throughout his body and required foot surgery. Tony could not walk and was confined to bed for all of those three months. The doctors were doubtful that he would survive. However, God had a different plan.

---

[18] Matthew 26:37–38

Something you need to know about my husband was that he loved life—I mean **loved** life. He was filled with joy and he knew how to give it away. And, he was a fighter. With God's miraculous intervention and Tony's fighting spirit, he amazingly survived the next five years. What a blessing! He believed in God's miracle power and was forever asking God, "When am I going to be healed so I can go back to work?"

As you may have guessed, this experience was very difficult for me. I was pulled into the grief cycle every time his health declined and then gained hope when he seemed to be gaining strength. It was a real yoyo experience. My heart felt like it was ripped apart and then stitched back together again and again and again. My body pain, of course, increased, because of the daily stress. Watching my husband, who was so active for the 47 years we were together, decline was very difficult. I was acclimated to my own illness and pain, but not used to seeing Tony's vitality trickle away.

I wanted my youthful husband back. I was angry, sad, heartbroken, and fearful that I wouldn't know how to go on without him. Because I was a child bride, all I knew was living my life with my companion, lover and best friend. I heard someone say, in one of the grief groups I attended, "Losing a mate is like losing an arm or a leg. It feels like there is a *part of you* that dies, not just another human being." I think that's a pretty accurate description.

At the beginning of Tony's five year illness, I moved my counseling office into my home so I could help care for him. He did not want to be in a nursing home and I wanted to try to honor that request. Outside of the stretches of time in the hospital we were able to make it work, although it was difficult. My children helped me a lot and I hired some aides towards the end of his time with us, but I carried the bulk of his care. It is something I really wanted to do; however, I was extremely exhausted, physically and emotionally. By the time he passed. I was so glad that my son, John, and I had made all the burial arrangements early in his illness. I couldn't imagine achieving that chore in the state I was in.

I did manage a wonderful celebration of life service for Tony, though, with the help of my children and the Holy Spirit. It was my deepest desire to deliver the eulogy and honor my husband in that way. My son John was my backup in case I couldn't make it through.

The viewing was the night before and my niece, Bette Marie, decided to sleep over so she could cook breakfast for me in the morning. Some of the family came back to the house and we talked about all the wonderful memories we had with Tony. There were so many. We cried and laughed and encouraged one another before bedtime. Bette Marie said, "Aunt Carol, I am just in the next room if you need me. You can wake me at any time." That was a very sweet gesture, but I and the rest of the household slept fine with God's grace.

When I awoke the next morning, my thoughts went right to my husband and the concern of having to say "good bye" to him today. I was very aware that I needed God's strength and Spirit to be with me. I began to formulate a prayer when all of a sudden this wonderful lavender mist began to fill my bedroom. It was beautiful! I had never seen anything like it. It was not only in the room, but the Lord was also filling my body with it. I felt the heaviness I had been carrying lift. I asked the Lord, "What does this mean?" He replied, "It is my peace."

I laid there for a while just soaking in this marvelous lavender mist. The depth of the peace I felt is impossible to describe. I felt my concerns of the day dissolve in this lovely mist from heaven. I *knew* that God was with me and I became aware that I was *now ready* for the day. I didn't move until I heard Bette Marie call out, "Breakfast is ready!"

When I joined her in the kitchen she seemed excited about something. I was anxious to tell her about my experience, although when I started describing the lavender light, she got so excited, she kept interrupting me. "No, I have to tell you this. I have to tell you what happened to me," she stammered.

Finally, when I decided to listen, she told me her experience:

> *When I woke up, I started praying for my family and for the day. While I was praying, a small lavender light came into my vision. I watched it get brighter and then bigger and bigger until the whole room was filled with this lavender light. I didn't know what it meant, but now I know.*

We both got so excited. God was making doubly sure that I got the message—His presence and His peace would be with me throughout the day. And it was.

I was so glad for that miraculous sign. It became a reminder to me that God was, without a doubt, with me. It impressed me so much that after I parted with Tony's things, I painted the bedroom lavender. God gives us these signs because He knows we need them.

My grief, naturally, has been up and down and all over the place. But there is always the comfort of Jesus, my faithful Savior. He continues to walk with me through the high times and low. He is faithful to show up with His miracles or His soft whispers to my heart. And, I embrace every act of love that my Lord extends to me. I am thankful, so very thankful that Jesus is who He says He is: faithful, loving, comforter, encourager, healer, deliverer, savior, redeemer, creator, almighty, eternal and supernatural God.

> *The eyes of the Lord are on the righteous, And His ears are open to their cry… The Lord is near to those who have a broken heart, And saves such as have a contrite spirit. (Psalm 34:15, 18 NKJ)*

Section III

Divine Purpose: Prepare

As my growth and maturity in Christ continued, Jesus took me on a journey of not only discovering what my calling was, but also teaching and gifting me for that calling. The first teaching was what I call "the school of the Holy Spirit" where He taught me how to move in the many gifts of the Spirit and how to pray and minister to the hearts of others. Here are some of the lessons I learned in some of the Christian conferences, spiritual retreats and ministry training classes I attended.

I received two years of ministry development training, MDT, at La Crescenta Foursquare Church and I earned a master's degree in Practical Ministry through Wagner Institute. At the Toronto Airport Fellowship Church I completed classes on moving in the prophetic with Graham Cooke and Mark Virkler and a number of classes on how to minister in the healing gifts. My skills continued to increase as did my amazement at the many ways Jesus touches and heals His people. During that span of time, I learned how to move in gifts of healing, deliverance, prophecy, and words of wisdom and knowledge.

As hungry as I was for more of the Lord, that's how hungry I became for more spiritual knowledge. Jesus was so faithful to lead me in the direction He wanted me to go and I am so thankful for all the pastors and teachers who imparted to me such valuable insight and biblical knowledge.

As you learned in Section I, it took awhile after my salvation experience for me to receive enough spiritual cleansing and inner healing to be able to minister to others. My soul healing was vital to fulfill God's plan for my life. This is a very important concept to understand. Ministry begins with a house cleaning of our temples first. We cannot give what we have not received. The two are tied together.

Can a dying tree bear fruit? Of course not; that is obvious. Although, sometimes we forget that and we try to minister to others out of an unhealed vessel. I don't propose that we have to be perfect, but we have to be healed enough so all our *stuff* doesn't block the Holy Spirit from moving through us.

In Section I and II, I talked about being primed for miracles through my hunger for more of God. That hunger needs to spill over and affect our calling as well. There should come a pressing into the fullness of what God designs to complete through us. The word that came to me was PREPARE. I have created a system to deepen your relationship with the Lord, using that as an acronym that we will look at throughout the chapters in this section.

Pray	=	Develop and grow a seasoned prayer life for self and others.
Repent	=	Where there is sin, be quick to repent and turn from it.
Expect	=	Expect God to do what He says He will do.
Press In	=	Don't let go of God or give up. Keep your eyes on the goal.
Aware	=	Be aware and aligned to what the Spirit is saying and doing.
Resurrect	=	Resurrect the new thing that God is doing in you.
Exercise	=	Exercise the gifts the Spirit is giving you. Use them.

This task is challenging, but living through the PREPARE system is always fulfilling. I guess I use that word often—fulfilling. I think it is because that is the word that best describes how I feel in my present walk and calling in the Lord. Isn't that the very best we can ask for—to feel filled? It is a deep feeling of satisfaction. I still would like to grow more and continue to be a part of God's working through me, but I am so glad that I can say, "I am presently deeply satisfied in the Lord." This satisfaction comes through knowing that I was always meant to be His child and as His child, was always meant to have a Divine purpose.

Each of you have a Divine purpose. Our journey is discovering what that is. God doesn't give us a road map. (I sometimes really wish He would!) However, He gives us enough pointers along the way to keep us from getting lost. So, let's look at PREPARE and see what pointers Jesus wants to give us through that system, to help us on this important journey.

> *"For I know the plans I have for you," says the Lord. "They are plans for good and not for disaster, to give you a future and a hope." (Jeremiah 29:11 NLT)*

Chapter Seventeen

Prayers of Intercession

The first P in PREPARE stands for Prayer.

As we begin this section on preparing for ministry, I have found that the greatest foundation for the work that the Lord wants to do through us is prayer. I was literally pulled, or better stated—yanked, into prayer by the Holy Spirit shortly after my miraculous encounter with Him. Prayer was essential in building my relationship with Jesus Christ, giving me vision for the journey ahead.

One of the first things that Jesus taught His disciples was how to pray.[19] There are many different kinds of prayers: prayers of praise, prayers of thanksgiving, prayers of blessing, prayers of petition, prayers of repentance, prayers of meditation, healing prayers, deliverance prayers and prayers of intercession.

The first kind of prayer the Lord led me into was intercessory prayer. Intercessory prayer is when we lift up the concern of others before the Lord and petition the Father to help. Interceding for others is a key element of ministry. It not only prepares our heart

---

[19] Matthew 6:9–13

to be a compassionate giver to that person, it also prepares the recipient's heart to be able to receive from the Holy Spirit.

> *Therefore confess your sins to each other and pray for each other so that you may be healed. The prayer of a righteous man is powerful and effective. (James 5:16 NIV)*

As I describe the ministry of intercessory prayer, I am going to share several components of prayer that are important. First, we must address God with a humble heart. Second, we must discover the burden on the heart of God and learn how to carry it with Him. In the process of explaining this second component, I will share a vision from God and explain how His burden became my calling.

Throughout my first decade of walking with the Lord, I was definitely called to a ministry of intercession. I could spend hours in prayer. My heart was so full of the concerns I had for my family and those people that I did not even know. From my living room the Holy Spirit led me to all parts of the world, filling me with wisdom to pray that could only have come from the heart of God.

This holy exchange stirred my heart and drew me further into His passions. I traveled down prayer paths where I could sense God's sadness over the fallen state of man, His burning desire for us to know His love and the depth of His grief over our pain. There were times when it was unnecessary to put words to my prayer. My heart said it all as I sat stilled by His enormous heart.

If you are thinking, "I don't hear God in that way when I intercede. Will my prayers get answered?" One thing I would like you to see is that God has many different ways to share His concerns with us. You may receive a specific image from Him or a dream. He may speak into your mind, as I noted in my experience, or He may give you an internal knowing or intuition of what to pray for. I found that many times I would start out praying for one thing and all of a sudden my prayer would go in a different direction. That is the Holy Spirit's guidance.

What is also true, is that even when you are going down a list of people and places to pray for, and you may not feel any strong directive from God, those prayers are heard by Him. As you will see, in my next story, the thing that concerns God the most as we pray is our heart.

Intercession is a holy calling in which the attitude of our hearts is primary. We need to remember that *it is the Lord who answers prayer* and He, alone, should gain the glory. Therefore, it is necessary that we come before Him in humility. If the heart's motivation is not pure, God will correct it, as He did me.

In this particular prayer season, I was led by God to fast (on liquids) for 40 days. I had been studying the scriptures on fasting[20] and learned how significant it could be to breaking strongholds of the enemy and ushering in the movement of the Spirit. Eager to follow God's directive, I said, "OK" and started into day one. I was amazed and thankful that I could even do it. Our church family usually fasted once a week, but nothing this extensive.

As the days passed, I noticed that a lot of my prayers were being answered and my excitement began to build. I was coming up on day 30 and I was overjoyed! I never felt so good in my body and spiritually I felt like I was touching heaven. The Holy Spirit had directed me to pray for church growth and salvations and both of these were manifested. I also interceded for some of the church leaders and they began to confess their struggles openly and received healing.

---

[20] Isaiah 58:6—9

I began to notice, however, that my ego was having great fun with this, too. I didn't say anything to anyone, but internally I felt like, "Hey, I'm doing a great job here! Wow, God must really be proud of me. Look at all the prayers I'm getting answered!"

Day 31 God slapped me on the hand. I knew He was telling me, "You think you are doing this? I want you to take notice." Quite suddenly, I lost all the ability to fast. I could almost hear the thud as I hit the earth. I *had* to eat and it was obvious that the fast was over. I became aware that the Holy Spirit had been giving me the grace to fast and He now was exercising His authority to withdraw His grace.

That was a difficult but memorable lesson. I needed to pay attention to what God was teaching me because He was leading me into a ministry of intercession and there was no place for my pride. Look at what the Gospel of Matthew has to say:

> *And now about prayer. When you pray, don't be like the hypocrites who love to pray publicly on the street corners and in the synagogues where everyone can see them. I assure you, that is all the reward they will ever get. But when you pray, go away by yourself, shut the door behind you, and pray to your Father secretly. Then your Father, who knows all secrets, will reward you. (Matthew 6:5–6 NLT)*

I don't think that the writer, here, is concerned with *where* we necessarily pray, but *how* we pray. Is your prayer a *humble* petition before God? What is *motivating* your prayer?

The other thing I needed to learn about prayer was that the Lord Jesus is the great intercessor. He is always bringing our concerns before the Father.[21] When we pray, we never pray alone.

---

[21] Hebrews 7:25

The Holy Spirit is directing and empowering our prayer[22] and Jesus is also praying with us before the Father. Jesus is the One who will carry our burdens if we let Him. The lesson is that *He* is the burden-bearer.

Burden: this is a word that is used rarely in today's culture, but it had a depth of meaning during biblical times. It means that Jesus can carry the weight of what concerns us if we look to Him to do so. Oxen were yoked together when plowing to make their job easier. So, also, we are to be yoked together with the Lord to make our task lighter—whether it is prayer, ministry or calling. Jesus tells us to cast off our own burdens and take on His. As we do this our burden becomes light.

Let me explain further. I do realize that whatever our burden is, *whatever* concern we are carrying on our hearts and minds, as we take it to the Lord, He joins with us and eases the weight of it. What I want you, also, to see, is that sometimes the specific burden that we are carrying God never meant for us to carry. We have put it on ourselves.

Jesus wants us to take that burden and cast it off and take up the burden that He gives us to carry. That burden will be light because it is a burden birthed by the Holy Spirit. The Holy Spirit knows what we are meant to be praying for, and what we are meant to be doing, so He is eager to join us in that endeavor. Our burden, then, is no longer our burden, but the Lord's, and therefore it is His to carry. Jesus instructs us:

> *Come to me, all you who are weary and burdened, and I will give you rest. Take* ***my yoke*** *upon you and learn from me, for I am gentle and humble in heart, and you will find rest for your souls. For* ***my yoke*** *is easy and* ***my***

---

[22] Romans 8:27

burden *is light. (Matthew 11:28–30 NIV, emphasis mine)*

This principle is also important to look at in regards to our calling. Our calling can be light or it can be heavy. If we are following our own path and not God's, I guarantee it will be heavy. It will be heavy because we will be carrying it on our own and not with Christ. The Lord used this next vision to illuminate that truth to me.

I was at a church meeting where there was an extended time allotted to intercession. I was on my face before the Lord, stretched out on the floor. At first, my head was busy. I was thinking about the teaching prior to this, although I made a concerted effort to focus on God as I waited for the Holy Spirit to direct me.

All of a sudden, I saw a sea of broken children. It was shocking. As far as my eyes could see—north, south, east and west—there were bodies of babies and young children. I could tell that they each were wounded or sick in some way. I asked the Lord, "What does this mean?"

In the next instant, my heart was wrenched inside of me. I could feel God's burden for these children. It was alarming. I don't think I ever felt that much pain. In that moment—God's heart and my heart were one. I could feel His overwhelming distress and anguish over the condition of His children. I laid there and wept with Him for the next hour.

When the burden began to lift, I asked Jesus, "What do you want me to do? What does this mean?" He said, "I am sending you to heal my wounded children, my children of all ages." I laid there for a while thinking about the commissioning of the Lord. It made sense because of other directives He had already given me. Nevertheless, this command was so pointed and clear. It was as if the hand of God reached in, grabbed my heart and yanked it into His chest.

"There is so much pain," I finally said to Him. "Yes, I know," He said. "Before I can send you, I must give you my heart. This is my heart, my burden, for the hurt and wounded."

I became silent for some time, until I got it. It became clear to me. This is God's burden, not mine. His work, not mine. The pain I felt in my heart was a good pain because it was an embodiment of God's love for the broken and it signaled to me that *He* would do the healing work that *His* heart was engaged in. I was much more aware that I was being invited into His work.

When I came away from that meeting, I knew that my heart was changed. I had already committed to school and was pursuing the degree I needed to follow my call to the wounded, but now I felt more grounded in that calling. My heart was radically impacted by God's loving heart for the broken. I now possessed heart knowledge and not just head knowledge to move me forward into the ministry God was giving me.

Today, I find I have a strong mission, therapeutically *and* spiritually, to those who have been broken through abuse of all kinds. I have studied various techniques for the treatment of trauma. And, I have completed a book, DVD teachings and workbook focused on abuse recovery called *Journey into Wholeness*. Through my years of schooling *and* through the impartation of God's heart (during the vision), my calling to pray and minister to the broken has remained strong and focused.

It may be difficult for you (in your humanity) to grasp the reality that Jesus wants *you* to partner with Him in prayer. As you take that leap, however, you will find God's heart leading you along into the plans He has for you. It is a wonderful journey! Remember, obtaining God's heart comes first, then the calling.

> *Trust in the Lord with all your heart; do not depend on your own understanding. Seek his will in all you do, and he will direct your paths. (Proverbs 3:5–6 NLT)*

Chapter Eighteen

Repentance

The first R in PREPARE is Repentence.

Do you know that God has a purpose, a plan, a calling for *your* life? Sometimes, we don't have a clue of what that is until we make the step to give our lives over to Him. Sometimes, our inborn natural gifts and abilities have already led us in a certain direction. Jesus can help you understand your passions and the journey that He has for you. Repentance may be part of the journey.

The simple definition of repentance is "to turn around"—to turn from the way we are walking and go in another direction. Sometimes God needs to turn us around before we can fulfill the calling He has for us. You will see how God needed to shift my plan 180 degrees, through repentence.

As a child and young adult my gifts led me into a career as a professional dancer. It was a dream I had since I was young and I pursued it with vigor. I traveled for a while with a tap dance troupe called The Manhattan Rockets and while a young adult owned a dance studio. It was a no-brainer. That was my calling, or at least I thought so until Jesus got a hold of my heart.

I received the Lord in 1975 and was still active in my dance studio. Within the next year, however, Jesus asked me to lay it down. At that moment I could not recognize what other plan He had for me, but I was confident that it was a good plan. As I shared in the beginning of this text, my conversion to Jesus, and the other miracles I experienced, were pretty radical and I was still basking in the amazing love and presence of God. Believing in God's goodness towards me, in a career change, was not something I had to question. After all He had done for me, "Why wouldn't He have something wonderful for me?"

I shared what I thought God was saying with my husband and he didn't share my enthusiasm. In fact, he thought I was crazy! He did not want me to close the studio. He had helped me build the studio and it was quite lucrative. Tony knew how much I loved dancing and it didn't make sense to him. We still had to learn God's ways and how to listen when He gives a directive.

I went to God with my dilemma. My husband was ready to put a large ad in the paper to bring in more students as the business had been dropping in numbers. I felt the reduction in students was the Lord's way of getting me ready to close, but my husband didn't want to hear it.

In prayer the Holy Spirit gave me an idea, "Tell your husband that if no one responds to the ad, that will be a sign to close." I thought, "That would have to be a miracle—first of all, every time I ran an advertisement there was enormous response, and second, how would my husband go for that?" He was pretty stubborn when he set his mind on something.

I ran the idea past my husband and he agreed to it. Wow! That was a shock. My second shock came when not one person answered the ad. I was convinced that God was directing me, even though I was amazed that He could actually give me that kind of sign. I was learning that God's ways were certainly not my ways and I closed the studio at the end of the school year in

June. I still didn't know where God was leading me, but I was learning how to trust.

That was my first miracle of many that positioned me into my calling today as therapist, teacher and author. I would never have guessed it in a million years, but I am so thankful I listened to God. Within the first year, following the closing of my school, I became very ill (which I explained to you in the first half). The timing for the closure was really the grace of God because I never could have had the stamina to complete my dancing career. Step by step, God was fashioning my path.

As I reflect on my experience, the biblical story I am reminded of is the narrative of Abraham. God gave Abraham a prophetic word that he would be the father of nations and that all the peoples of the earth would be blessed through him.[23] That is a pretty magnificent promise I would say. But wait! Look what the Lord required of him:

> *The Lord said to Abram, "Leave your country, your people and your father's household and go to the land I will show you." (Genesis 12:1 NIV)*

I didn't know where God was taking me. I didn't see that in the future I would return to school and become a therapist. I didn't see that I would minister to others through healing prayer. I didn't see that I would be sitting here, right now, writing words of encouragement to you. God has a plan for us even when we can't see the plan. Furthermore, it is always a good plan that will bring fulfillment and blessing.

Since I have walked with the Lord for four decades, I have learned something about Him. He often directs us to give

---

[23] Genesis 12:2–3

something up in order to gain something else. First of all, that is often necessary for movement to happen. We, humans, can become quite content with the status-quo. And, in that place, we can lose the vision and possibility of something else.

There was another thing God needed to change in me, however, for the marvelous plan He had for me to be fulfilled. Dance, He revealed, had become my idol. I am still so thankful that dance, in my young years, was my salvation. When I felt alone or afraid, I would go down to our basement and dance. It was another whole world where there was no abuse—just me and my music and dance. Nevertheless, without my knowledge, it had woven its way into my heart and soul as my ego identity. I was a dancer. That's who I was!

Jesus knew that that part of my identity needed transformation. I am a child of God first, then everything else follows after it. Or, I should say, everything else comes *out of* who I am in Jesus Christ. Ministry comes *out of* my relationship with Jesus Christ—as does calling and career. Jesus Christ has to be at the center, or the path we choose may not be the best plan.

Learning to let go is a good thing. Everything we have on this earth is a gift. We don't have to grip it with closed fist. The image I like is: standing before God with an open hand, allowing the thing God gives us to just rest in the palm. It is from that position that Jesus can move us freely according to His plan and direction.

When Jesus revealed to me how tightly I was holding on to my identity as a dancer and that it was getting in the way of the greater thing He had for me, my first response was grief—not the grief over having to let go of my dream—but, the grief over my desire to hold onto something that was opposed to God and His plan. This is *good* grief—the grief that can lead us to repentance when we are not aligned with God. God had shown me so much of His love that I didn't want to act contrary to Him. I must say that I didn't fully understand, but my heart understood the truth that I had made dance an idol. Therefore, I repented of the idol I had fashioned and made the choice to give dance to Him.

The greatest part of my experience is that Jesus did not have to rip dance from my hand. I am thankful that He revealed His love to me and gave me the grace to understand that this was His goodness extended to me, even though I could not see where He was taking me. I am thankful that I listened to Him, but I do not take the credit for my ability to follow it through. It was sincerely the wonderful grace that is engendered by the Holy Spirit when we make the choice. Repentance requires that we turn around; however, the power of the Spirit comes to help us once we make the choice.

So, I want to ask you the question, "Are you holding on to something that the Lord wants to transform? Is the Lord asking you to change direction?" Repentance can open a door to a path you never imagined. He is a good God who has good things for you.

This is Jesus speaking:

> *Those who love their life in this world will lose it. Those who despise their life in this world will keep it for eternal life. All those who want to be my disciples must come and follow me, because my servants must be where I am. And if they follow me, the Father will honor them. (John 12:25–26 NLT)*

Chapter Nineteen

Expectation

The first E in PREPARE is for Expectation.

As I explained in Sections I and II, my relationship with God was heavily influenced by the impact of the miraculous. My supernatural experiences definitely propelled my faith and boosted my spirituality. Those experiences are what I counted on to sustain me. My expectations of how God would act towards me, were mainly influenced by those miraculous encounters.

As my walk with the Lord developed, however, my expectations became increasingly based on the character of God. I still believe in God's ability to act towards me in supernatural ways; nevertheless, I now recognize that it is God's *goodness*, which is housed inside those miracles, that is the important thing. I may still get disappointed if God acts in a way that is contrary to my expectations, but it doesn't have the ability to rock my faith in the goodness of God.

> *Let us hold fast the confession of our hope without wavering, for He who promised is faithful. (Hebrews 10:23 NKJ)*

God is a big God who can act in any number of ways to display His love to us. The more that we expand our vision of God—through our experiences *and* through His Word—the more our expectations of Him can expand. This lesson is really only taught over time. Here is my experience during my second decade of walking with the Lord.

Between the ages of 30–40 years old, Jesus continued teaching and healing me. He was also gifting me and revealing His plans for my life. I was released in my church to pray for many people in the area of inner healing and deliverance. People started telling me, "You are so good at this. Why don't you go to school and become a therapist?" You do know that God can speak to us through other people?

Anyway, in time I had to take notice of what they were saying. I had left my career in dance and I wasn't trained for any other kind of work. However, there were several glitches in that school idea. Number one, I was still battling the body pain associated with the fibromyalgia. Number two, I would need *a lot* of school.

I had dropped out of High School to dance, so I didn't even have a High School Diploma. To become a Marriage and Family Therapist I would need a BA in psychology and a MA in Marriage and Family Therapy. That would be a total of six years if I had the energy to go straight through.

I did a lot of praying during that time and Jesus confirmed His plan step by step. The most important confirmation was the peace I was experiencing concerning my career move. I remembered a teaching I had back in the beginning of my walk with the Lord. The premise of the teaching was, "Peace in your heart can be sign that God is leading you." Another important validation came through my husband who affirmed my idea and would support my decision. We had financial issues we would have to work on together, but there I was, at age 40, heading back to school.

I started at the community college level with two classes my first semester. They had a wonderful handicap aid program on campus, which I took advantage of. Since walking was difficult for me (especially on the hilly campus), they had small motorized carts that transported me from one class to another. If I wasn't able to make class, I just needed to call in and they would audio tape the class.

There were many mini-miracles like that throughout my six and a half years of school, and the next five years of internship and acquiring my state license. My expectation—that God would see me through—was challenged many times, but the Holy Spirit gave me the grace to stay on course. There were many times He came and picked *me* up. This next story was one of those times.

As I have shared with you, my body pain continued throughout my early Christian experience. Since I had already experienced the miracle power of God, I believed that getting free of this illness was a no brainer. I began my vigilante attack against this illness through prayer and fasting. I received prayer whenever it was offered with the expectation that God would heal me.

When it was obvious that God was not answering my prayers, I took a second step and started to search out and attend every healing meeting I could find. I remember leaving many of the healing meetings in tears, overwhelmed by disappointment and feelings of rejection. Gradually, resentments towards God were beginning to harden my heart.

I finally determined that God was trying to teach me something in the pain-filled place where I found myself and I made a "grit your teeth" decision to somehow do what I needed to do to move forward with God. I was convinced that if I waited on God's timing and learned what I was supposed to learn, that God would heal me. Surely that was the lesson! It was my expectation, certainly.

Many years passed in my seemingly endless cycles of belief, anticipation and then despair. I know that some of what kept me engaged in that cycle was my own fleshy tenacity and determination to be healed. I hadn't uncovered the truth yet that we can't dictate to God when and how our miracle will happen or if it will happen. The end result was my heart grew cold towards God.

Oh, I suppose if you asked me, "Do you believe in God?" I would have said, "Yes." But, the deeper heart issue was that I had stopped believing that God *loved me*. I don't think I could have voiced that at the time. I just knew I was done trying to please God. But God had a hidden agenda, and a miracle to share.

The set-up was ingenious. (Of course, God is greater than a genius, so I wouldn't expect anything less!) I was attending college, working on my Bachelors. And, of course, I had picked a Christian college that *happened* to require all students to attend chapel three times a week. Most of the time it wasn't a problem. I mindlessly sat through the service without the shield around my heart being punctured. This day was different, however.

I didn't notice anything new as I walked into the room. It was a little warm and I felt a little tired. But, there was no signal to me that everything, in my internal state, was about to make a 360 degree change. We sang the usual three worship choruses and the guest pastor was introduced as he walked to the podium.

Until that day, I had never heard of Father Brennan Manning. I did not know that he was passionate about the love of God and that most of his books and teachings were focused on just that. I did recognize, though, that there was something compelling about him—something that was drawing me to listen to him. Here is my account of that happening as I related it in my book, *Meditations from the River:*

God's Deliberate Pursuit of Me

I cannot remember the date or the title of the pastor's message, but I vividly remember that he spoke directly into my spirit and soul. His words captivated my heart and stirred it awake from a long deep sleep. In some ways it was as though I was hearing those words for the first time in my life as this slightly built priest leaned over the pulpit and with magnetic force bellowed out, "Abba, your Father, has an extravagant love for you."

He measured out that phrase several more times with equal magnetism and I soon realized that the only thing my senses were attuned to was the pastor, Abba Father, and me. Time held no relevance; neither did the faces around me, nor the knowledge that chapel would soon be over and I would have to return to class. The only notable occurrence was the shift inside my own body, spirit and soul. Years of pain had programmed my heart not to feel, and now it was responding to the beckoning of the Spirit's call.

The breaking open of my heart was sweet. Abba (the Hebrew word for "Daddy") was befriending the heart that had turned from Him for so many years. It was my misperception that He had deserted me through my physical trials (like my childhood abandonment by my dad and grandma), when in reality, it was my heart that had grown inattentive. I paused in that holy moment and noticed that my heart was now turned toward Him—stilled by such an amazing extravagant love. (p. 58)

The shield that I had erected around my heart was shattered in seconds. The love of God was far greater. Yes, I had to choose to turn back to Him, but how else could I respond to His real, vibrant, passionate, enormous love. I remember that moment as if it were yesterday. It was God calling me, wooing me into His heart of forgiveness and grace. God had a hidden agenda for me that day and it included a miracle.

God's miracles come in many different shapes and sizes. At times it may be difficult to assess a *happening* as supernatural. Although, I can assure you, if you haven't made a logical concerted effort to change, and suddenly your heart and direction in your life has radically changed, you can bet it is a God miracle.

In my work as a therapist, I am intrigued, as I meet people in all kinds of differing, yet painful, circumstances that God is creative enough to meet each one in the way that *they* need. If I were watching for *my* expectation, I might determine that God didn't show up. The miracle that I was looking for, that day in chapel, was not my first choice, but looking at it now, it was the best choice. Jesus knew what I really needed was a heart adjustment and not a physical adjustment.

To follow Jesus, we must become visionaries. In my therapy office I have had to learn to flow with the movement of the Holy Spirit. I may have an idea of where God is leading, but rigidly following *my* idea may not accomplish what God intended. God's intention requires our expectations to shift at times.

In my personal life, as I grow and mature in the Lord, my expectations can shift more readily. I can trust where God is leading me because I can better trust His motives. Focusing on God's character helps me to see the big picture—that He is a good God who has a good plan for my life. That doesn't mean that I should stop having specific expectations of God. Remembering the truth of our relationship frees me up to easily shift direction when guided.

Jesus knew that my heart had to turn around if I was to complete the calling He set out for me. My expectation (that God's initial agenda would be to heal me physically) had to shift so that I could see the goodness of God and His plan for me.

> *Then I heard the Lord asking, "Whom should I send as a messenger to my people? Who will go for us?" And I said, "Lord, I'll go! Send me." (Isaiah 6:8 NLT)*

Chapter Twenty

Press In

Press In is the next lesson as we PREPARE.

Has God placed a dream in your heart—a calling—but somehow it has gotten derailed by life? The most difficult part about *pressing in* to what God has for us, is keeping the dream alive when it seems like *time* and *life events* have intruded upon the goal. Doubts can come creeping into our minds about God, "Did God really give me that dream?" or about ourselves, "Did I understand right? Am I good enough?"

I believe one of the most difficult lessons we have to learn and apply is that moving towards our calling is a journey, not a three hour jet ride to a one-stop destination. This is how the Apostle Paul explains this lesson:

> *Not that I have already obtained all this, or have already been made perfect, but I press on to take hold of that for which Christ Jesus took hold of me. Brothers, I do not consider myself yet to have taken hold of it. But one thing I do. Forgetting what is behind and straining*

> *toward what is ahead, I press on toward the goal to win the prize for which God has called me heavenward in Christ Jesus. (Philippians 3:12–14 NIV)*

So, what is the goal? The ultimate goal, as we see in the scripture above, is being transformed into the image of God and receiving our heavenly rewards when we see Jesus face to face. But, the goal also includes our calling—the ministry on earth we are called to complete.

Before giving my life to Jesus Christ my dream was becoming a dancer, and I pursued it with all my heart and might. Once I discovered my higher calling, however, I pursued my new path. It was easy to shift my attention, but it was a lot of joyful, focused work to move forward. I attended six and a half years of school, completed my license as a Marriage and Family Therapist, got established in my private practice, formed a prayer ministry training lay counselors, finished the manuscripts of two books and was looking forward to the adventure of publishing, marketing them and sharing my work through public speaking.

After so many years of pushing through the academics and, at the same time, struggling with my physical challenges, I was really excited about where I had come, and anticipated new adventures ahead of me. It felt like I was on the threshold of a new season in which I would see some of God's plans for my life come to fruition.

Then, everything I had been working towards for the Lord stopped short. The next season was dark and difficult, anything but fulfilling. My husband became critically ill with cancer and heart disease. Determined to care for him at home, I shifted my busy practice to my home office to care for him in between clients. At the same time, my mom was declining with Alzheimers. My days were filled with visiting my mom at the nursing home, watching the life drain from her body and mind, driving home in tears, and pulling myself together to cook and help my husband to bed.

My own health was compromised as well. I contracted Lyme's disease and for three months it was necessary to hook myself up twice daily to antibiotic IVs. I still managed to see a limited amount of clients in my clinical practice, but had little energy left for ministry and ended that work. My books were still not published, and I began doubting their value—or probably it is more accurate to say *my* value.

Because of the grief I was processing and the disappointment that this season brought, it was difficult, at times, to keep my emotions from despair. It is so easy to get blinded to the big picture that God holds in His mind when we are challenged to this degree. Some days my only prayer was, "Jesus, help me."

In the middle of my distress, my friend Christy called and invited me to a church meeting one night. I really didn't feel up to going, but pushed myself out the door. I am so glad that I did because the Lord extended a miracle to me that night in the form of a prophetic word.

One thing that the gracious Lord often does to keep us on track, is repeat His promise to us. He repeated His promise to Abraham and Sarah *many* times throughout their lives concerning the child that they would have.[24] When they birthed the child, Abraham was 100 years old and Sarah was 90.[25]

I, too, have been blessed with receiving prophetic words that confirmed to me that I was traveling in the right direction. Prophecy is God speaking His plans to us either through a dream, vision, speaking into our hearts, speaking through His Word or speaking through other people.

---

[24] Genesis 12:3, 13:16, 15:4, 17:1–5, 16, 19, 21, 18:10
[25] Genesis 17:17, 21:2

There were many different prophecies I received at key points in my life where I needed a boost to keep on going. This example had a specific significance to me. It was delivered to me during this difficult season when I was doubting myself and my ministry. I needed a shift to open my mind and heart and Christy's invitation came at the perfect time. Here was the prophetic word given to me at Harvest Rock Church, January 2010:

> *Earlier when we were prophesying over other people I heard the word "mother" and then I saw these very large wings. Once again, we are told not to interpret, but I saw mother and wings. And, I feel the Lord has probably already brought a lot of people to you, but I believe He is expanding your territory, your tent. And, these wings are not little wings—they were these huge massive wings. So, I feel that you can encompass a lot more, take care of a lot more than you have. He's going to bring in a lot of people that you are going to mother. You are going to be a safe place where they can come. You are going to release wisdom into their lives and you are going to bring structure and bring the nurturing that they so desperately need.*
>
> *I sense that you hang on and press into God and that there is something in particular that you want from Him. He is saying that He is delaying for no other reason except a timing factor. Everything has divine timing. You are one that is like a bull dog—you just won't let go and you grab hold. And, He's saying He's the one who is holding the other side. He knows the timing and it's going to be perfect. I don't have a clue what **it** is, but I really feel that God is in*

it. Do not grow weary for in due season you are going to reap more than what you expect. There is really going to be glory in that. There is really going to be a breath of fresh air.

I feel like this has been heavy on your heart. Because of your tenacity (you just won't let go) it's been kind of a burden that He wants to begin to release from you because He wants you to come into a place of joy. He is saying, "It is done!" It is done in the spiritual realm and in the natural it will come in the perfect time. So, do not grow weary. Let go and trust.

I have a picture for you that you saw for me. I saw a rose that was full and open and in its maturity. I just sense that there is a wonderful richness and a maturity of things that God has grown in your life—a rich storehouse of things that you have to give away. And, it is not a limited supply, but things that the Lord has brought into fullness in your own life and a richness that you will give out to others.

I feel like there is grace on your life for publishing. I feel like the Lord is going to have you publish in the area that God is showing you and teaching you in the Spirit. And, that there is grace for multiplication and distribution. There are other places (I don't know if they are clinics or what there are), but other people are going to want these things. So, don't feel like, "This is just for me, just for what I am doing." There are other people who are hungry for that healing and the spirit of counsel that is on your life—which you are going to publish. You are going to publish the good news. But, it's to be

> *multiplied and there are other places that will seek it out. They are going to long for it. So, there is a grace gift on it. The Lord wants you to know not to hold back in your gift. He's going to show you and lead you in the details because there are other places that need it, too.*

The speaker, part of a visiting ministry team to my church, did not know me or any of the details of my life. She did not know that I was a counselor and that I was also in the process of writing recovery materials for publication. And she didn't know that I was growing weary.

The wonderful thing was that Jesus knew all of that and He knew just how to speak to me and give me hope. Up until that day, I thought I had somehow missed what God wanted me to do. But here, Jesus was telling me that He was going to bring it to pass in His time. I hadn't missed it! I just needed to keep going and know that He was blessing it.

I have learned repeatedly that in the middle of distress, we need to stay connected to each other in the body of Christ because in doing so we can gain hope through giving and receiving encouraging words. Yes, the Lord did meet me day by day in the brief moments I had to spend with Him. Each day, I fought to keep my hunger for the Lord alive even though it felt as though I was dragging my heart along.

I want you to know that practicing our faith as best we can is often enough to help us keep pressing in. Doing the spiritual behaviors that worked in the past—reading the Word of God, spending time with the Lord in prayer, worshipping, reminding ourselves of His blessings—all those things can keep us connected to God and on the path He set before us even when our hearts may be struggling to keep up the pace.

As I stated previously, "I love the instantaneous miracles." But that is not all our walk with the Lord consists of. *Pressing in* involves exercising our faith on the mountain tops and through the valleys. A relationship with Jesus is a day by day growth experience. You may find it difficult, as I did, to *press in* towards the Lord while encountering a crisis that has uprooted your plan. My experience has been that Jesus will meet us when we need Him, if we do.

I exercised my newfound hope by contacting a publisher to self-publish my book and I worked on materials for a set of teaching DVDs that would go with my book and workbook. I can't say it was a quick work, in between all my other obligations, but I kept praying for God's leading and kept writing. The one thing hopelessness does is stop us in our tracks and keeps us from completing the work God has set before us. That is the enemy. God's plan for me was to keep believing and keep writing.

That God-given prophecy was so up-lifting. It gave me hope and empowered me to keep moving forward and not give up. God's Word tells us that this is what New Testament prophecy is supposed to do:

> *But everyone who prophesies speaks to men for their strengthening, encouragement and comfort. (1 Corinthians 14:3 NIV)*

Even now, as I reflect on this prophecy, it is a great reminder that God is not only aware of all the details of my life, but He is also **in** all the details. I encourage those of you who have received prophecies to write them down and meditate on them. It is always a good idea to keep a spiritual journal where you can write the things that God is speaking to you through His Word, through times of prayer and reflection and through prophetic utterances.

Pressing in involves gaining the vision that God has for our lives and trusting that God will get us there in His time and way. It includes keeping our eyes on the goal and continuing the forward momentum, even when we cannot yet see the fruit. And, it includes learning how to listen when Jesus speaks and, once we hear, to allow His words to go deep into our soul and become a part of us—to strengthen and encourage us in our journey of *pressing into* every good thing that God has for us.

> *For if we are faithful to the end, trusting God just as firmly as when we first believed, we will share in all that belongs to Christ. (Hebrews 3:14 NLT)*

Chapter Twenty-One

Be Aware

The A of PREPARE is a call to be Aware and Aligned to what Spirit is saying or doing.

What a privilege God has given us! When we are called by His Spirit to follow Him and we say *Yes,* the Holy Spirit actually comes into our hearts and lives inside us. We become spiritually alive and, as such, can consider ourselves to be agents of the supernatural. Just as the Holy Spirit reached out and touched our hearts, He can now touch others through us. We now have a *supernatural calling* to spread the Kingdom of our God to this earth.

I have already established that a miracle is God reaching to us, into our time and space, revealing who He is and in so doing releases His Kingdom (a new way of being) to this earth. But, another amazing fact is that through Christ's marvelous resurrection and ascension, the same miraculous power of the Holy Spirit that He possessed was released to us!

We, frail human beings, are also bearers of His Kingdom if we are aware of this gift. We can be the instruments through which supernatural healing, deliverance, signs and wonders can be released to others on this earth giving testimony to who Christ is and His love for us. These are Jesus' words:

> *You will receive power when the Holy Spirit comes on you; and you will be my witnesses in Jerusalem, and in all Judea and Samaria, and to the ends of the earth. (Acts 1:8 NIV)*

The Holy Spirit gifts each one of us in differing ways. Sometimes He gifts us with a certain gift just because it is what is needed at the time. For instance, my husband, Tony, shared the gift of physical healing more than I did. I shared emotional healing more than him. However, if there was someone coming to me for physical healing, and God decided to heal the person at that time, the Holy Spirit could move through me with what that individual needed.

Nevertheless, each individual is usually gifted with and functions in certain gifts that line up with their callings. I have shared gifts of prophecy, words of wisdom and knowledge, emotional and inner healing, and deliverance. There are many gifts, but the same Holy Spirit.[26] That is why the Spirit can act according to the need.

It is up to us to become *aware* of what the Holy Spirit is saying and doing. That is a skill that takes time to learn. It can be enhanced through spending intimate time with Jesus and the Holy Spirit, and listening from stillness to what they are saying. The more you use the gifts given, the more skilled you will become.

Within my learning season, the Lord gave me many opportunities to practice. I call them my mini-mission trips. My

---

[26] 1 Corinthians 12: 6–11

excursions started out as retreats to refresh my spirit. I enjoyed getting away from the house, family and obligations to spend time alone in prayer and restoration. Of course, the Holy Spirit often had a different plan in mind and I had to learn to put my agenda aside to follow the Lord's.

One particular retreat, I was driving down to Palm Springs. A friend lent me their rental home for a few days and I welcomed the opportunity. As I was driving, I had my ear turned towards the Lord. I usually don't play music in the car because I like to use that time to commune with God. There was an excitement growing inside of me and I was eager to hear from God about what He had for me.

Then I heard in my heart, "I want you to get off at the next rest stop. There is someone there whom I want you to pray with and encourage." I was fairly used to God springing these miracle visits on me and, as I watched for the turn out, I prayed that God would show me the person right away.

I made the turn and parked in an area where there were several tables. The rest area was almost completely deserted, but the Lord directed me to just sit and wait. After a while, a young boy started heading towards me from across the park. He looked about seven years old and was engaged in waving a tree branch through the air and marking a path beneath him. As soon as he reached me, he asked me my name. I told him, "My name is Carol. What's your name?" He told me it was Jim.

I began to wonder if Jim was the person I was to pray with, when his mom started calling him and walked over. She was plainly dressed in jeans and sweat shirt. She wore no makeup and her hair was a bit unkept. I introduced myself to her, but she seemed a little cautious to speak with me. She had difficulty making eye contact with me. Without looking up, in a soft voice she said, "My name is Gail."

I asked her if her and her son were hungry. Gail hesitated. I said, "It is not a problem to me. I have some extra sandwiches and fruit in my car if she would like." She said a simple, "Yes." So, I went to my car and gathered the food together from my cooler.

When I got back to the picnic table, I laid some paper towel down as placemats and handed Gail and Jim the sandwiches, fruit and two sodas. As they sat eating, I told her my story, and shared that God had sent me there to her. "He wants you to know that He is with you." She got very teary and said, "It's been a long time since I've been in church." I told her that it's not about being in church. "God wants you to know He loves you right where you are." Her face was softening, but I could tell that it was very hard for her to take it in.

I sat with Gail for the next hour while she poured out some of her pain and I gave her some suggestions where her and her son could go for food and shelter. When I asked her if she would like prayer, she was eager for it. I could tell that God was blessing her in the midst of the prayer and when I was finished, she was actually smiling. I asked her if I could give her a hug, which she welcomed. I gave Gail a small money gift, assured her that she and her son would be in my prayers and left.

As I pulled away, I was so thankful that God could use me in that way. I am amazed every time it happens. Please remember that you can be the vehicle to deliver a miracle to somebody today. All it takes is letting the Lord know that you are available for a supernatural adventure and being *aware* when the Spirit leads you.

Throughout my growth in the Lord, I developed more and more awareness of the gifts of the Spirit He was imparting to me. I am so thankful for all of the gifts, but especially the gift of deliverance. I think it is especially exciting to me because it enables me to view, first hand, the power of God to set His children free of demonic oppression. To see the effects of someone hopelessly immobilized by the enemy, and then witness their freedom and joy when the Spirit of God moves, thrills my heart beyond measure.

Because deliverance was such a key to my personal healing, it feels natural and normal to be able to minister in that way to others. Discerning of spirits, which is a crucial part of ministering deliverance, is also necessary in intercessional prayer, where the Lord continued to lead me. That is what my next retreat experience was about (although the Lord did not reveal that ahead of time!)

After spending some time prayer, I felt led by God to a convent, which was located about a two hour drive from my home. The online description sounded perfect. It was a home tucked away in the mountains surrounded by plenty of hiking trails and streams. I wanted to be able to sit and write some, so I also requested a room with ample windows and light.

When I arrived at this retreat house, I discovered that the house itself was an ancient castle. It had a dark ominous feel to it and as I exited the car and made my way to the massive front door, I felt uneasy. I was trying to talk myself out of getting creeped out, "Carol, this just reminds you of some old movies. Don't make a big deal out of it."

A pleasant nun opened the door and helped me find my room. She gave me all the particulars: the times for common dining, meditation and evening prayers. I was feeling a little more comfortable and after unpacking I decided to go to their meditation room and pray.

The room was comfortable enough. It had large pillows for kneeling or sitting and large windows, which brought a beautiful view of the woodsy hillsides. When I knelt to pray, though, my mind was bombarded as it had never been before. I was so confused that I couldn't even focus on a prayer. My thoughts were swirling inside of my head. I decided to pray in tongues to see if that would clear my mind. It did not.

I realized very quickly that this was demonic oppression and the probable reason why Jesus had sent me to this place. My goals of rest and refreshment had to be put aside. I went for a walk through the building to see if I could get a clue as to what I was battling. Throughout the hallways I found myriads of books and artifacts from other religions and spiritual pursuits. Jesus Christ was definitely not revered as God, but merely one of the many gods presented.

Before dinner I asked to use their phone. I had determined that I needed prayer assistance if I was going to stay and do this work. I was relieved that my prayer partner was available. It was no surprise that she was already interceding on my behalf. I related to her what I felt we would be praying against and she committed to intercede with me.

The Lord led me to go to evening prayers and there I got a clear view of some of the demonic entities that were ruling in this place. I was alerted, in my spirit, that there were spirits of idolatry, worship of false gods and rebellion against Jesus. The Lord also began giving me a burden to pray for those in this community who were being deceived. My heart was beginning to feel the weight of sorrow that Jesus felt as he looked on them. I went to my room and wept and prayed for them.

As I began to wage war against the enemy (binding their power in Jesus name), the darkness closed in upon my body. I was used to dealing with the demonic, but this weight of sin I had not experienced. I continued to pray as the Holy Spirit directed me, but I was also battling the lies of the enemy, "If you stay here, I will surely kill you."

I did not stop praying for hours, although now I was beginning to feel weak and sick in my body. Something startled me and I looked up and saw a dark figure over me with a dagger in his hand. The Spirit was showing me that this was a very real danger. My body literally began shaking and I immediately asked the Lord for a sign if I was to stay. I was fairly used to praying against demonic oppression, but I also wanted to make a rational decision, with the Lord, if I was to stay or not. That is when I saw two powerful angels outside my door.

The door, itself, was huge, but these magnificent creatures were a head taller than the door. I could see that they were clothed in full battle armor with swords at their sides. They were positioned on either side of the door facing out and their posture was one of alertness. I knew that my Jesus had placed them there to protect me. As soon as I saw them, a great peace swept over me. The shaking in my body ceased. This was the confirmation from God that I needed to stay.

I spent the next few days praying, as I walked through the building and grounds, declaring the Lordship of Jesus Christ over the land. The Holy Spirit was faithful to show me how to pray and break the enemy ties that this order of nuns had unknowingly opened themselves up to. I felt like the Lord was reestablishing the plans that He had for this property and this group of people. There would be more work that the Spirit of God would have to do, although finally I felt my part was done. On the third day I began to feel that extreme weakness and fatigue again. I knew it was time to leave.

As I drove home, I prayed prayers of thanksgiving for what God was doing in that small religious community. As always, I thanked Him for using me. It is not only a privilege, but it is also exciting to get a peek into the spiritual realm. My faith was strengthened as well as my gifts. I worshipped and praised God all the way home. God is an amazing God. This encounter with the miraculous proved that to me again.

You may not understand this kind of gifting in the Spirit. You may be meant to share a different gift or maybe you do not yet know what gift the Spirit is imparting to you. But, I want to encourage you to become aware of the Holy Spirit and enlarge your capacity to listen to Him. There are spiritual adventures He desires to lead you on as well.

> *Now there are different kinds of spiritual gifts, but it is the same Holy Spirit who is the*

source of them all... There are different ways God works in our lives, but it is the same God who does the work through all of us. A spiritual gift is given to each of us as a means of helping the entire church. (I Corinthians 12:4, 6–7 NLT)

Chapter Twenty-Two

Resurrect

The second R in PREPARE stands for Resurrect.

God is continually calling us to resurrect the new thing that He is doing in us. That is because, if we let Him, God is always doing a new thing in us. As you can tell from my story, I am not in the habit of staying in one place for very long. I have learned to get excited about the next discovery that the Lord is leading me into. That is also part of my "more" theology.

There is always more that the Lord wants to reveal to us of Himself and the awesome wonderful plans He has for us. So, I want to ask you this question, "How hungry are you?" I am not just enquiring about your heart, as you seek after more of God, but also as you seek the gifts and calling that He wants to impart to you and through you.

Jesus has sent us, you and me, into this world to transform this world—to resurrect it—to bring life, His life, to a dead and dying people. Why else would He send us His Spirit, His gifts, His power and His love? We are to receive it *and* give it away.

The vision that I am about to share with you emphasized that truth to my heart and propelled me into a healing ministry.

This is one of those wow experiences, a big miracle to match a big God. I would like you to look inside the vision with me to recognize the calling He was placing on me. I said earlier that miracles come to us for all kinds of reasons. It can be easy to get caught up in the wow and miss the message. That is especially true of this vision because of its magnitude. I am going to try and slow down and pull apart various sections to let you know what I believe God was communicating to me.

This vision came at a very transitional time for me. I had just completed collage and I was beginning my internship at California Christian Counseling Center. I was blessed to get the exact internship that I wanted. I was feeling a lot more settled since the pressure of school was over, but I still had to complete 3,000 hours of counseling before taking state boards. All in all, though, I was feeling pretty good about myself and where I was going.

I celebrated my milestone by going to my favorite church in Toronto. They were having a four day conference on the "Love of God" and I was ready to get filled up once again. As was my norm, I began to fast and pray and prepare my heart for what God had for me. My prayer was always the same, "Whatever you have for me, Lord, that's what I want. If there is any part of my heart that doesn't agree, please change my heart." It seems to be a prayer that the Holy Spirit likes because He leads me into it quite frequently.

The church service hadn't begun yet, but everyone was mulling around—chatting, praying for one another, checking out the book store items, purchasing water or snacks for the service or lying on the floor meditating. I could feel the presence of God already. That is why people would hang out for hours in the sanctuary. It was always filled with a very warm loving presence of the Spirit. My favorite position was lying on the floor with my attention fixed on the Lord, which I found so easy to do in that sweet Holy Spirit presence. It was from this church that I learned how to meditate and it was a practice I took home with me. The focus is on *taking in* from God—His love, care and healing presence.

The worship was about to begin and everyone was finding their seats or places for worship. A whole group of people went up to the large area surrounding the front platform. They usually stayed on their feet the whole time, jumping, dancing and waving arms or banners. Once in a while I would try that, but my body usually gave out before my spirit.

This time I felt compelled to find a spot along the wall where I could lie down. From the moment I positioned myself on the floor, the weight of the Holy Spirit was on me and I began to think about the resurrection of Christ. Through the years I had received so much new life from Christ—resurrection life. What would the Lord impart to me today? I knew the career I was heading into—counseling others—was God directed, although I really wanted Christ's power and life to flow through it. I was so aware that change could not come to me or those I ministered to without the power of the living Christ.

I had been transformed in so many areas of my being through faith in Christ's resurrection. And, here I was again, seeking, asking, knocking for something more. The worship time was glorious and I remained there as well through the preaching. The presence of God was so thick, I didn't want to move. At ministry time someone reached down to pray for me and the weight of the Spirit became heavier. I didn't know what God was doing, but I was willing to wait.

At some point my senses were totally taken up by the Spirit. My friend tried to arouse me and when she couldn't, she left a note under my head letting me know where she would be. One moment I was lying there soaking up the love of God and the next moment my spiritual eyes became flooded with the brightness of God as He began to open heaven before me. It was like the layers that separated earth and heaven were being pealed back, allowing more and more brilliance to enter my vision.

It was obvious, immediately, that I was in the throne room of God. My eyes were drawn to a figure sitting on the throne, though I couldn't differentiate His features. The worship that was happening contained voices and sounds I have never heard on earth. This glorious sound not only filled the atmosphere, it seemed to become a part of the atmosphere—like the air itself was singing. As I continued to lie there, my spirit and soul were caught up and became one with the heavenly worship.

Everything I pictured in the throne room was white. The massive stairs leading up to the throne were some kind of white marble, as was the throne itself. However, they weren't just white. They seemed to be filled with and radiate the very brilliance and splendor of God, Himself.

My attention then turned to a river that seemed to be flowing out from the center of the throne. It was perfectly clear and it, too, radiated light. What amazed me about the river was that it was like looking into a beautiful sparkling emerald. (The Lord showed me later that the emerald represented His mercy.)

As I lay there, I began to notice that I, too, was immersed in the glorious healing waters. I had a deep knowing that His river was flowing through every part of my body bringing vitality to every cell. My body, soul and spirit were so thirsty, they seemed to keep drinking more and more. Mesmerized, I could not move. I did not want to move. I longed to stay there for eternity.

In a while, my awareness shifted back to the throne room stairs where I noticed that the stairs were filled with the saints. All of them were on their knees and all were worshipping. In their hands they held golden bowls. Inside the bowls I could see sparklers like the kind you would hold on the 4th of July! That made me really curious and I asked the Lord, "What are the sparklers?" He said, "Those sparklers are the prayers of my people."

When He said that, the saints poured the contents of their bowls into the river and the river began to effervesce and swell.

It was as if the river came alive in response to the prayers. I was captivated as I watched the river then spill over the edge of heaven and down into and across the earth. I started thinking, "This is how our prayers bring healing waters to the earth."

Just then, a golden chariot, carrying our resurrected Christ, flew into the throne room. There were two massive white horses pulling it and the back was filled with billowing fire. Jesus stepped out of the chariot and as He did, a thunderous praise came forth from everywhere. Yet again, I was caught up into this majestic moment.

The Christ then started taking handfuls of fire from the chariot and thrusting them into the river. He had the authority to do that because He had overcome hell, death and the grave. The river was quickly ablaze. He said, "This fire is the life of my Holy Spirit."

Jesus was sending His Spirit to bring resurrection life to the earth. I was overcome with the knowledge that Jesus makes a way for us to know Him and know His love.

I remained fascinated by my heavenly vision when I heard, "Carol, come up here." Instantaneously, there was a mixture of emotions that came up inside of me. I was excited and overwhelmed, but somewhat fearful. I thought, "Am I worthy to walk up those stairs? What will the Lord say or do once I got there?" I really was content to just lie on my face before Him. I heard Him say, again, "Carol, don't be afraid. I want you to come up here."

So, I lifted my head and walked up the glorious stairway. I stopped directly in front of my Lord where I stood with my head down. He said, "Carol, would you lift your head and look at me?" As He spoke that, He gently put His hand under my chin and lifted my head.

I was stunned. There was fire flashing from His eyes. Jesus said, "Look into my eyes." When I did, His love, my Savior's love that was grander than anything I had ever experienced or imagined, penetrated my being. What was unique about this moment was that in the fire, I could feel both His passion and His strength. His love is not a flimsy whimsical love. It is a love that is filled with *intent*. It is a love birthed through His death and resurrection. Jesus' passion for me, for us, is strong and intentional. We are the object of His fiery love.

In that moment I felt worthy—not worthy because of who I was, but worthy because of who He is. I became so aware of the cross and the price He paid for me. I am worthy because of His loving sacrifice for me. When His fire penetrated my being, I knew in that moment that He knew me, every part of me, but His love for me eradicated my failure.

His love for us is pure. It is not deluded with outside affections. It is like an archer whose arrow hits his target. We are the target. We are the objects of God's intentional strong unwavering love.

As I stood beside Him, He took another handful of fire and touched it to my ears, eyes, mouth, heart and hands. Jesus said, "I am sending you to my people, but I am sending my Holy Spirit to go with you. He will cause you to hear my words, see my revelations, speak my truth, go where my heart leads you, and bring healing through your hands."

I heard Him speak again, "This redeeming work is my work, not yours. But, I have chosen you to be a part of it."

I remained in the Spirit and in His river for some time soaking in His love and His words. When I got up I wasn't the same. That is God's resurrection power! I always had had a heart to serve the Lord, though now I possessed a deep passionate fiery enthusiasm to do so. I knew deep in my heart that He was sending me and that He wasn't sending me alone. I had a strong conviction that this was His work and all I had to do was follow Him.

Following this vision, Jesus birthed a *new* ministry through me called Rivers of Mercy Ministry. Of course I named it after the healing river coming from the throne. We did once a month healing conferences where I taught on God's design to heal us, as well as having prayer for the sick. God blessed many of the participants with physical and emotional healing and miracles.

This was an exciting time for me as God was confirming that His calling for me was not just for the counseling office. He was broadening my vision. There were spiritual gifts He was giving me to bless the body of Christ. It was also an exciting time because Tony and I had an opportunity to minister together. Tony had a heart for evangelism and for physical healing, so he was a great asset to the team. It was a very unique time as we got to see the extraordinary resurrection power of God flowing through us. When you step into that place, it is so exhilarating and yet so humbling. Will you step into the river today and resurrect what God wants to do through you?

> *For if we have been united together in the likeness of His death, certainly we also shall be in the likeness of His resurrection… And do not present your members as instruments of unrighteousness to sin, but present yourselves to God as being alive from the dead, and your members as instruments of righteousness to God. (Romans 6:5, 13 NKJ)*

Chapter Twenty-Three

Exercise

Here we are, at the last E of PREPARE, Exercise.

God grants us the gifts supernaturally, but we need to learn how to use them. That skill is achieved through exercise—*using* the gifts God gives you.

As I continued to grow in the Lord, learn of Him and have my character molded by Him, gifts of the Spirit began to be manifested. I was also blessed to be in a church that embraced and taught their leaders how to operate in the gifts. It was not surprising that deliverance was one of the gifts that I seemed to function in the most. In the first half of this book, I shared how deliverance from the demonic was an important part of my emotional healing. Often, the same healing that we have received from the Lord can be passed on through us.

Jesus kept bringing me people who were in need of deliverance and the pastor, recognizing my gift, also channeled those in need to me. I was working at California Christian Counseling Center, completing my internship for Marriage and Family Therapist, when I experienced this next event I'm about to share with you.

One of the reasons I picked that counseling center for my internship is that they wholeheartedly embraced Christian disciplines along side clinical therapeutic techniques. That was what the Lord had been teaching me and I was glad to be able to practice in a place that understood that. It promotes so much healing for the individual when both of those disciplines, the spiritual and the psychological, can function together. You will see, in this next example, how functioning in the spiritual and psychological was vitally important.

My client schedule was usually quite full. Some days literally felt like a revolving door. This day had started out that way. I saw two clients back to back and this was my third coming in. She was a woman I had seen quite regularly for some time. I will call her Mary to protect her privacy.

Mary took her usual seat on the sofa and I on the high back armed chair. We exchanged some pleasantries and I opened the session in prayer. I closed my eyes, bowed my head and prayed a very simple prayer, "Dear Jesus, you know what you have for Mary today, so I pray that you would help us to line up with your will for her."

I opened my eyes and realized right away that Mary was not sitting in her chair. I looked down and thought, "Oh my!" Mary was lying flat on the floor, wiggling like a snake, with her tongue darting in and out of her mouth. Now, this was not exactly what I had in mind for today!

I recognized immediately that this must be a demonic manifestation. My next thought was, "Is this what you want to do today, Lord?" What a silly question! If this is not what God had in mind for today, then what? My next thought was, "Do I have enough time for this?" Looking at Mary, I determined, "This might not be a one session deal." I ran through my schedule in my head and was pretty sure there was no one in the next slot, so I decided to start praying to see what this was all about.

I prayed and talked with Mary and prayed some more before we got through the layers of sin that created an open door for the enemy. As it turned out, there was a boat-load of resentments and bitternesses she held towards her husband which manifested in her cursing at and belittling him. Most of the work I had to do was inviting the healing of God into each area of pain, where she was wounded by her husband, and helping her to see where she needed to repent and let go of the bitterness.

An easy formula to remember when praying to break a stronghold of the enemy is: Repent, Renounce, and Break. *Repent* of the sin that opened the door to the enemy. Repenting is to God. For Mary, it was confessing the resentments towards her husband and her wrong actions towards him. Renouncing refers to Satan, the enemy. Mary needed to declare to the enemy that bitterness will no longer be a part of her. Breaking takes the authority that was given to us by Christ and, as His servants, to break the power of the enemy over that area. When the heart is turned around, then deliverance is easy. The enemy has to listen to us because of what Christ did on the cross.

Once Mary decided that that sin was not going to rule her anymore, than it was easy for me to take authority over the enemy and command him to leave. Jesus Christ, the Deliverer, moved that day and Mary was set free. I give you this example, not to lift up the enemy, although this example gives us a clear picture of how the enemy seeks to gain control. The miracle working power of God was present and when she got her heart turned towards Him, He instantaneously set Mary free.

It is clear, when reading the accounts of Jesus' ministry, that deliverance was very much a part of what He did. And, He repeatedly told His disciples to do the same. However, as we look at this next scripture reference, you will see the warning that Jesus gives to His followers concerning the gifts and especially the gift of deliverance.

In Luke 10, we find the account of Jesus directing seventy-two of His followers to go out ahead of Him, preach and heal the sick. When they returned, look at what they said:

> *The seventy-two returned with joy and said, "Lord, even the demons submit to us in your name." He replied, "I saw Satan fall like lightning from heaven. I have given you authority to trample on snakes and scorpions and to overcome all the power of the enemy; nothing will harm you. However, do not rejoice that the spirits submit to you, but rejoice that your names are written in heaven." (Luke 10:17–20 NIV)*

Jesus' statement points us back to the greatest miracle of all and that is the gift of salvation. It is so tempting in our flesh to get excited when we see miracles happen and even for our egos to get puffed up. But, we need to remember, "It is all about Jesus. He is the one who gives us the power. *He* is the deliverer."

I would also like you to remember that there are many ways in which Jesus delivers us. The above example is the bells and whistles miracle. However, deliverance begins in the heart when we choose to turn from our own way and yield to the Holy Spirit. It is a matter of setting our *will* to line up with God's will for us, and exercise our gifts in service of Him.

That is the thing I have to remember as I counsel or minister to others—everyone has free will. I may be able to point someone to Christ or into a path of healing, but they alone have to choose to accept or reject it. That is the place where it is important to get out of the way and let the Holy Spirit have His way. I used to say, "The Holy Spirit is my co-therapist," when in actuality, He is the lead therapist and I am the co-therapist. Therefore, part of learning how to move in the gifts of the Spirit is learning when to get out of the way.

In a *super* supernatural happening, sometimes I just stand back and watch. You will see that in my next client example, Sherry-Anne. When I share her story with you, notice the creative way Jesus came and integrated her psyche. Yes, there was a lot of work that she and the Holy Spirit had to do prior to the integration, but in God's timing, He reached in and designed something new. As someone who had been working with her for some time, I was so excited for her. I had witnessed her step by step progress and was eager to jump out of the way and see Jesus work a miracle.

Jesus knows what small steps are necessary to bring us into the big picture. Sometimes, He only reveals the process piece by piece if He knows we would be overwhelmed or not comprehend the big picture. Most of the time, that is how I view my calling as a therapist. Jesus might reveal to me the big picture, but it is my job to help the individual walk step by step into that plan.

Yes, God's plan for my client, Sherry-Anne, included a creative miracle. I will let her tell her story:

> *Hi my name is Sherry-Anne and I am 40 years old. I was in college when I started to have memories of my childhood abuse. My prayer was, "God I feel so broken. Show me and rebuild me the way you always wanted me to be." I struggled with depression, severe health issues and I often wanted to commit suicide. My father took his life at age 38 and I didn't want that outcome for myself. I was desperate to be free. This was the beginning of my almost 18 year journey of healing.*
>
> *My first marriage was abusive and as I married for the second time we moved from Australia to US for my husband's work. After three years, my husband came to me and said, "I*

don't know what to do. You are not remembering things that you have said or done or sometimes things that I have said." I was scared and I felt like I was going crazy. I prayed that God would give me a counselor to help me.

I was given Carol's name by a friend at church and went to see her. The first time I went for an appointment, we talked and she gave me a book to read on DID, Dissociative Identity Disorder. As I read the book, I found myself in each and every page. I was relieved to know what it was. Now I wanted to know how I could get well.

It wasn't a quick fix, but I also never knew that I would encounter Jesus' and the Father's love in such a tangible way through my healing journey. After spending several sessions working with Carol, I became aware of several personalities that I possessed. Each part had different interests and was good at different things, and I started to understand how things worked in my internal world. However, we found that the system was breaking down and the dissociation that had helped me as a child (to live through incredible trauma) was not helping me as an adult. God wanted to heal me, but it would be a journey of patience—learning to love and embrace all the parts of me. I love this scripture:

For the Son of Man has come to seek and to save that which was lost. (Luke 19:10 NKJ)

> *One of the most memorable occasions for me (and the most miraculous) was at an appointment with Carol. As she led me in a prayer, I could see the three parts of me that were still dissociated. I saw Jesus meeting us and we all held hands. At that point, Jesus gave each part time to process the specific pain they carried. Then it was time for all of them to be integrated.*
>
> *This was a special moment where Jesus brought all of us into one. I was amazed that all those parts were returned to me. Later, after driving home, I went for a walk on the boardwalk by the ocean. It was the first time that I could clearly see the color of the water and sky. It was a beautiful vivid color. And, I could smell and sense everything around me. I felt like I was alive for the first time!*
>
> *I was so thankful to be a whole person with no separate parts. I would still continue my journey with Jesus, although now I would do it as one person. (Used by permission)*

As we follow together with the Lord, into our various callings, it is always amazing to me how the Lord executes our individual paths. He not only has knowledge of where He is taking us, but also provides the ways in which we get there. He can maneuver the right people into our path to help us and if we get off track, He knows exactly how to get us to adjust our ways.

Jesus knew exactly where He was taking Sherry-Anne. Yes, it involved a lot of twists and turns, but He was faithful. I was so blessed to play my part in her recovery, but even more blessed to have witnessed God's amazing miracle in her life. I recognize the awesome privilege of joining together with God's Spirit to see the miraculous flow to others. That is a privilege I am willing to *exercise* to maintain and grow.

As you can see from the two examples I used in this chapter, there are sometimes very different ways to move in the gifts of the Spirit. Jesus is a willing teacher, but it does take time to learn how to listen and to join with the Holy Spirit in the supernatural flow for that individual.

My encouragement to you is to *use* the gifts God gives you. In so doing, you will be an intimate witness to His amazing works. Try not to be inhibited by fear or unworthiness. Remember, *Jesus* is the Healer and Deliverer. He is the One who is supernatural. You are the witness.

> *Now glory be to God! By his mighty power at work within us, he is able to accomplish infinitely more than we would ever dare to ask or hope. (Ephesians 3:20 NLT)*

Epilogue

As I come to the conclusion of this book, I have many mixed feelings. The first thing that I feel is gratitude. I am so aware that God has rained His goodness down on me in so many ways. I am aware of the deep dark places He rescued me from. And I am aware of His bigness. It is my earnest hope that you gleaned some of that awareness, as well, as you pondered my miraculous experiences.

I feel full. Satisfied. When we tell our life stories, there is something incredible that happens on the inside. While studying some of the theory and works of Daniel J. Siegel, M. D., I learned of his marvelous theory regarding our life stories. It has to do with how our brain organizes and unifies our past experiences with the present and creates a whole narrative. His conclusion was that it is not so much the hurt and trauma we went through in the past that determines our health in the present, but it is how we *process* the pain that is the determinant. In his book, *Mindsight*, he writes:

> When we are able to "make sense" of our lives in a deep, integrative manner, what emerges is a coherent narrative of our lives. (p. 74)

> "Coherent narratives"—the way we make sense of our lives and free ourselves from the

> *prisons of the past—are an important predictor of relational health. (p. 70)*

When we add to that knowledge the insight and transformation that the Spirit brings to us, we can compile a powerful narrative of our ever changing lives. The past pain becomes rich soil for our character growth. The beauty of writing the narrative is that sometimes we have to take a deeper look at the trials and notice how they link to the successes.

That is true for me, in this writing. I have come to recognize more fully the many big and little ways God has worked to bring me to wholeness. The cohesiveness that I am experiencing in my spirit and soul is deeply recognizable. And, even though I don't see the end yet, I am assured that the transforming and integrative work of the Holy Spirit will continue throughout the rest of my life.

If you would like to write a narrative of your journey, a good place to start is by journaling daily. Try to include your feelings and responses throughout your daily events and not just the events themselves. Forming a narrative is all about you learning about yourself—who you are—including thoughts, feelings, aspirations. Also include your interactions with others and especially your interactions with the Lord. What is He speaking or revealing to you?

You can use my story as a blueprint revealing the kinds of experiences you might focus on. Please remember, though, that we are all different individuals with uniquely diverse stories. Another pointer, as you begin to write, try and write freely without paying attention to grammar or spelling. The main goal is self-exploration.

Life is an amazing journey of hills and valleys which can bring us to the destination that God has planned for us if we look to Him. God is always aware of the big picture and writing a narrative helps *us* to gain *His* view. Especially when we have been in the valley for a while, or we feel stuck in the pain of the past, a fresh look at how all of those ups and downs help to complete us, can bring us hope. Jesus has promised us that He can take *everything* in our lives and work it together for our good.

> *And we know that God causes everything to work together for the good of those who love God and are called according to his purpose for them. (Romans 8:28 NLT)*

This last miracle I am about to share with you is a miracle that is exceptionally special to my heart, one that unfolded in many ways through my personal journals as I learned and grew. For as long as I have known the Lord and known how to pray, I have prayed for a healthy heart attitude towards my mom. I prayed. I fasted and prayed. I confessed my faults to others and had them pray. It seemed like nothing radically changed the resentments and fear that entrapped my heart.

I knew how to behave properly with my mom, although there were many times when everything built up on the inside and the ugliness pushed its' way out. I hated my behavior then. I felt bad for my mom and I felt huge amounts of guilt and shame for myself. After these outbursts, I often went deep into *serious* prayer. But again, my heart would not budge.

It wasn't until I got into therapy myself that some of the mystery surrounding this issue came to light. My mother had high anxiety and a disorder called Obsessive Compulsive Disorder. She was never formally diagnosed with this disorder, but it became very obvious to me that it was what she suffered from. And, I came to realize that some of my actions towards her were *re*actions to some of the seemingly intrusive rituals that she had.

As a child I hated my mother's eyes. I felt continually watched and, in fact, I was. I was her obsessive object and she was going to make sure I dressed right, looked right and behaved right. Right, of course, meant whatever felt *right* to her obsessive thinking. My anxiety skyrocketed on the inside, but I learned how to make the outside attend to mom's standards. As a child, teen and even a young adult, I had no idea that my resentments were, for the most part, attributed to her disease and not her. All I knew was that I ached on the inside for it to be different. I wish I could have known that at the end of her life we would experience the most glorious healing we could ever imagine.

Mom was diagnosed with Alzheimer's Disease in her early 70's. At first the disease progressed rather slowly. She was able to move herself from New York to California where we lived. We, also, had time to move her into a senior living facility that she thoroughly enjoyed for several years before the severe dementia set in. That was a great blessing. However, I never could have guessed that the greatest blessing would come in her final months with us.

The Alzheimers followed a predicted course. Her memory continued to slip away and her grasp on reality. One personal blessing, to me, was that she always knew I was her daughter and she always knew my name. (I always felt that was "a God thing" especially as the Alzheimers progressed.) When I would walk into the common dining area to visit her, she would say, "Oh, my daughter Carol."

In her last months, though, her speech was minimal. It was then that we learned how to talk with our eyes. What a work of God! The very thing that repulsed me, throughout my life, my mother's eyes—became the very thing I was drawn to. It seemed like, as the dementia progressed, the defenses, which held the OCD traits in place, were gradually stripped away. What was left was my mom's pure love.

She could touch me without my wanting to withdraw. I came to love her presence and I loved touching her. Even though she couldn't speak, I would look into her eyes and sincerely tell her all the things I longed to say for years, but couldn't. I call this a miracle because it was a miracle. Every time I was with her, my heart healed more and more. And, I know her heart was healing, too. The sweetness that was happening between us was palpable. People would notice and comment on it. Here is one of my journal entries I wrote during that time:

> *Thank you, Lord, for the little (Big) miracles! Friday, visiting with my mom was a gift. I loved seeing her peaceful and happy. I recognized that she was happy because I was with her. The miracle was—that I could take it in. I don't know if the Lord is transforming my heart (I asked for that) or if it is because my mother's anxiety is not as present. I don't feel consumed or trapped by her.*
>
> *It was sweet, sitting there watching the program at the nursing home, holding my mother's hand. It felt comfortable and warm and genuine. Maybe that's what her love is really like underneath the fears and defenses. What a gift! Thank you, God, for that moment when I could take in the genuine love from my mother's heart.*
>
> *A picture popped into my mind of fireflies. We used to have them in the East and I would catch them and put them into a (vented) jar until the jar was flittering with light. That moment with my mother was like that—a flashing moment where I could catch the light of her love and place it in my heart. Maybe if there are enough of those moments, joy will return to my heart—a flittering, exciting, heartwarming light of joy. Thank you, Mama.*

This day was pivotal in God's miraculous healing of my heart. We had so many days like that, my mom and I. The last three weeks of her life, when she could no longer speak at all, we talked solely with our eyes. We said so much to one another during that time. I felt like it made up for a life-time. What a gift God gave us! The healing miraculously washed all the negativity in our relationship away. Now, when I think of her, I think of her love. It was so present, so sweet, so pure, so amazing, so big, so miraculous. Today, I have no thoughts that are marred by the past traumas with her. There is just love. This is the word of God:

> *Then I will give them one heart, and I will put a new spirit within them, and take the stony heart out of their flesh, and give them a heart of flesh. (Ezekiel 11: 19 NKJ)*

This is the way my heart feels. It feels new, brand-new. There are no half healed places poking their pain into the present. It was done. In an instant, God gave me a new heart—a heart of flesh towards my mama. I gained a heart that could feel her love and a heart that could give love to her. After so many years of wrestling with my heart, it was done.

I can easily say that outside of my salvation, this is the biggest miracle God has given me. There are no words to express my gratitude. That is why I dedicate this book to her. It is my thankfulness to her for opening her heart and making this miracle from God available to both of us. Thank you, again, Mama.

This miracle also reminds me that, **"It is never too late for a miracle."** I thought sure that this one was not going to be answered on this earth, but God had a marvelous surprise for me. He may have a wonderful surprise waiting for you, too.

Our healing journey with the Lord is progressive. It is progressive in the sense that when we have opened our hearts to the Lord, for Him to do a transformative work, that *opening* makes our hearts more available for the next move of God. Each choice that we make, to submit to God, creates a pathway for the higher purposes of God to be worked in our lives.

As I have said so many times in this writing, "God always has more for us." He has more healing, more miracles, more comfort, more revelation, more of *Himself* to impart to us. The way we make room for the "more" is by opening our hearts. That is the key towards becoming the whole healed individuals God intends us to be.

So, say, "Yes." Say, "Yes" to the Lord when He knocks on the door to your heart. Maybe you'll be opening your heart for the first time. Maybe this will be your one-hundredth time or your one-thousandth time. He is always knocking. He always has more.

I am so grateful that you have given me this opportunity to share my story, and speak into your life. We do need one another for encouragement, inspiration and guidance. I pray that this experience has produced those things in you.

SCRIPTURE REFERENCES

Scripture quotations marked NKJ are from:
The Spirit-Filled Life Bible, New King James Version. ©1991 by Thomas Nelson, Inc. (Used by permission. All rights reserved.)

Scripture quotations marked NLT are from:
The Life Recovery Bible, New Living Translation. ©1998 by Tyndale House Publishers, Inc., Wheaton, IL 60189. (Used by permission. All rights reserved.)

Scripture quotations marked NIV are from:
The Thompson Chain-Reference Bible, New International Version. ©1983 by B.B.
Kirkbride Bible Company, Inc., Indianapolis, Indiana and Zondervan Bible Publishers, Grand Rapids, Michigan. (Used by permission. All rights reserved.)

References

Chapter Five:
Omartian, Stormie. *Stormie.* Eugene, Oregon: Harvest House Publishers, 1986.

Chapter Seven:
Basham, Don. *Deliver Me From Evil.* Ada, Michigan: Chosen Books, Baker Publishing Group. 1972.
Hammond, Frank and Ida Mae. *Pigs In The Parlor.* Kirkwood, Missouri: Impact Books, 1973.

Chapter Eight:
Cohen, Lewis, Berzoff, Joan, & Elin, Mark, eds., *Dissociative Identity Disorder.* Northvale, New Jersey: Jason Aronson, Inc., 1995.
Romeo, Carol. *Meditations From The River.* Bloomington, Indiana: AuthorHouse, 2008.

Chapter Nine:
Keating, Thomas. *Invitation to Love.* NY, NY: Continuum Publishing Company, 2003.

Chapter Eleven:
Chevreau, Guy. *Catch The Fire.* Toronto, Canada: First Canadian Harper Perennial, 1995.

Chapter Twelve:
Coutinho, Fr. Paul. *How Big is Your God?* Chicago, Illinois: Loyola Press, 2007.

Chapter Fourteen:
Baker, Heidi and Rolland. *Always Enough,* Grand Rapids, Michigan: Chosen Books, 2003.

Chapter Fifteen:
Metaxas, Eric. *Miracles.* NY, NY: Dutton, 2014.

Chapter Eighteen:
Romeo, Carol, *Meditations From The River.* Bloomington, Indiana: AuthorHouse, 2008.

Section IV:
Kubler-Ross, Elizabeth. *On Death and Dying.* NY, NY: Scribner, 2011.

Epilogue:
Siegel, Daniel J., M.D. *Mindsight.* NY, NY: Bantam Books, 2010.

About the Author

Carol Romeo is a seasoned author, speaker, and marriage and family therapist. She has crafted five books throughout the past 2 decades of serving others with the accumulated wisdom that she gained throughout her personal recovery process and her experience counseling others. Carol received her bachelor's degree in psychology and her master's degree in marriage and family therapy from Azusa Pacific University. Carol feels passionate about her goal to bring wounded people to health and is convinced that it is vital to include spiritual training as part of the healing. This understanding moved her to gain a master's degree of practical ministry from Wagner Leadership Institute and functioned as a prayer counselor in numerous churches.

While thinking about how I want to present myself and my works to you, I was reminded by the Lord that the contents of my books are really a journey. First of all, they are **my** journey. Each book describes my struggles during that part of my life and how the Lord healed, delivered me and ushered me into a **new me**. This is a process whose stages are dictated by Christ and Him alone. It is a process designed for each of us individually because He alone knows our needs and what we need from Him to transform us into the **new whole** persons we were meant to be.

Books authored by Carol Romeo

Meditations from the River: Healing Waters for Troubled Times. Copyright 2008 by Carol Romeo. AuthorHouse Publishing, Bloomington, Indiana.

Traveling with the Life-Giver: A Spiritual Journey Through Recovery from Abuse. Copyright 2012 by Carol Romeo. AuthorHouse Publishing, Bloomington, Indiana.

Expect the Miraculous: A True Life Story of the Extraordinary Power of God. Copyright 2017 by Carol Romeo. WestBow Press, Bloomington, Indiana.

Be a Powerful Woman of God: A Testament of His Goodness. Copyright 2021 by Carol Romeo. Trilogy Christian Publishing, Tustin, California

Journey into Wholeness: Steps to Emotional Wholeness. Copyright 2022 by Carol Romeo. Brilliant Books, San Francisco, California

www.ingramcontent.com/pod-product-compliance
Lightning Source LLC
Chambersburg PA
CBHW060356080526
44583CB00012B/339